Happiness for Busy Professionals

Achieving Balance, Peace and Fulfillment in a Fast-Paced World

HAPPINESS
GRATITUDE
THANKFULLNESS

Happiness for Busy Professionals

Achieving Balance, Peace and Fulfillment in a Fast-Paced World

Dr. Mandeep Sharma

walnutpublication.com

INDIA • UK • USA

Paperback ISBN: 978-93-48945-49-5
eBook ISBN: 978-93-48945-71-6

First Published on December 2025

Published by Walnut Publication

(an imprint of Vyusta Platforms Private Limited)

www.walnutpublication.com

India

Unit# 909, 9th Floor, Wave Silver Tower, Sector-18, Noida - 201301

UK

71-75 Shelton Street, Covent Garden, London, WC2H 9JQ, UK

Distributed by

ZopioTail

I'm honored to offer this mini-handbook, *Happiness for Busy Professionals*, as a small gift of gratitude to the people and places that have quietly shaped my journey.

First, to my wife, **Shilpa**. You have been my anchor and my sunshine. Your love has not only filled my life with joy, it has also given me the courage to pursue work that serves others. To my children, **Ishanay and Aarnav**: thank you for being my closest companions, my honest critics, and the gentle reminder that the best kind of happiness is found in everyday moments together.

To my parents, **Shri R.K. Sharma** and **Smt. Rita Sharma**: I carry your values with me in everything I do. Your unconditional support, discipline, and compassion have been my lifelong foundation. If this book carries any steadiness, warmth, or sincerity, it is because you taught me to live those qualities first.

To my younger brother, **Sahdeep**: thank you for your quiet strength and constant belief. Your presence has always been reassuring, even when words were not needed. Your creativity and dedication have also added a special touch to this book, and I am proud to share that with readers.

I also bow with deep respect and gratitude to my mentor and coach, **Late Col. Ravindar Popli (Retd.)**. Your guidance left an imprint on my leadership and on my life. The lessons you gave me, about integrity, courage, and humility, continue to guide my choices every day.

Finally, my sincere thanks to **Nokia**, an organization I have been privileged to be part of for nearly two decades. It has given me room to grow, challenge myself, and serve with purpose. I am especially grateful for the space and trust that allowed me to bring a "happy working" approach into my professional life and to practice coaching as a leadership style.

If this book helps you pause, breathe, and reclaim even a little more joy in your daily life, then it will have fulfilled its purpose.

Advance Praise

What Leaders & Experts Are Saying About *Happiness for Busy Professionals*

"A timely and impactful guide for busy leaders. Leaders are the prime movers of building happier workplaces, and this book delivers highly practical advice."

Dr. Antarpreet Singh

Director (Academics) – Executive Education, Indian School of Business (ISB) | IIM-Indore | Chief Learning Officer | Professor AI-HRM | Chair – Executive Education

"Sharma avoids abstract discussion and offers tools that are immediately useful, while staying psychologically and philosophically grounded."

Dr. Rajeev Sharma

Dean Academics, Mangalayatan University

"A rare balance of scientific grounding and soulful guidance. The 'Quick Actionables' feel like a coaching session that fits a busy schedule."

Dr. Disha Shah

(MPT, PhD (Sch.), IFMCP (USA)

Founder & Director, Mission Health & Anaaham

"The clarity and depth of Sharma's writing offer not only valuable insights but also practical tools that are easy to implement. The book made me realize that happiness is not something to chase, but something to create in the midst of our busy lives. Dr. Sharma has condensed decades of experience and research into a reader-friendly guide."

Dr. Ritika Popli

Assistant Professor, Department of Writing & Rhetoric, Colgate University, USA

Trusted by Professionals Across Industry & Academia

"Refreshing and transformational. Every professional struggling with stress, burnout, or balance should read this. The mindset section alone is worth it."

Ashwani Khillan

COO, ALTIUS

"Dr. Mandeep takes us from the understanding and pursuit of happiness to the elements that truly shape it: daily habits, emotions, relationships, life purpose, designing an environment of joy, work-life balance, and sustainable self-care. The *Happiness Compass* brings it all together as a powerful inner framework for busy professionals."

Gopa Kumar

Chief Executive Officer, Ranext Technologies

"I approached it with curiosity and found genuine inspiration. It balances practical advice with deep reflection—this is what makes it stand out."

CA P. K. Jain

Chartered Accountant & Entrepreneur, Delhi (NCR)

"Each chapter feels like a coaching session—clear and deeply practical. The blend of Eastern wisdom with Western research is excellent."

Dr. Sidharth Jain

Professor, Institute of Business Management & Commerce, MU, Aligarh

"Equally scientific and soulful. Warm, people-connected writing that doesn't preach—it empowers."

Neeraj Sharma

Senior Leader & Business Head, Lovely Sweets & Bake Studio

Preface

In today's relentlessly paced world, it's not uncommon to meet high-achieving professionals who seem to have it all—successful careers, recognition, and influence—yet quietly struggle with an unsettling question:

"Why don't we feel truly happy?"

I've asked myself that same question.

This book was born out of my personal quest—both as a professional who has spent decades in the corporate world as a people's leader and as a certified coach deeply invested in human growth and well-being. Over the years, I've interacted with thousands of talented individuals—leaders, managers, engineers, executives, and experts—across the industry and multiple cultures. And while their journeys looked impressive on paper, a surprising number of them felt **mentally fatigued, emotionally isolated, and spiritually adrift.**

Not because they lacked success, but because they had lost sight of what **happiness really meant to them**.

Why This Book, Why Now

Happiness for Busy Professionals is not another book filled with generic tips or abstract philosophy. It is a **practical, relatable, and deeply human guide** for professionals who are juggling ambition and overload—and are ready to create more meaning, joy, and emotional clarity in their lives.

You've likely read other books on happiness. Perhaps you've attended webinars or listened to TED Talks. And yet, many of those resources either lean too far into superficial "feel-good" tactics or dive too deeply into academic theory, without bridging the two.

This book is different.

It distils **decades of real-world leadership experience, science-backed coaching insights**, and **a deep understanding of modern professional challenges** into a **clear, actionable framework**—designed to fit into the lives of people who are smart, stretched, and short on time.

What You'll Find Inside

Each chapter in this book offers:

- A **core concept** rooted in both research and real-world relevance
- **Engaging stories and relatable reflections**
- **Quick-action tools**, coaching prompts, and rituals that take minutes—not hours
- Illustrations and frameworks that simplify complexity

You'll explore topics like:

- Mindset shifts that boost happiness even during high-pressure periods
- Rituals that spark joy in the middle of chaotic workdays
- Why time management isn't enough—and how **value-aligned scheduling** changes everything
- The science of relationships, rest, purpose, and self-renewal
- A complete, customized **personal happiness system** by the end of the book

Who This Is For

This book is written for busy professionals and highly engaged leaders like you:

- Those who are **successful but tired**
- Those who have **read a lot but need simplicity and personalization**
- Those who want to stop waiting for happiness "someday" and start living with joy **now**

Whether you're a busy corporate executive, leader, entrepreneur, professional, educator, or high-functioning parent—this book respects your intelligence, your time, and your desire for authenticity.

My Personal Why

This book is not a theoretical exercise—it's a deeply personal mission.

I have seen friends, customers, and colleagues go through life **checking boxes but missing fulfillment**. I've experienced moments of internal struggle beneath external accomplishments. And I know how elusive happiness can feel when you're caught in the rhythm of relentless responsibility.

That's why I wrote this book:

To offer clarity where there's confusion.

To offer renewal where there's fatigue.

To offer a map—not to some abstract destination, but to your own **inner compass** for living better.

If you commit just a few minutes a day to this book, and apply even **one insight per chapter**, I'm confident it will shift how you experience your work, your time, your relationships—and most importantly, **yourself**.

Let's rediscover happiness—not as a reward for burning out—but as a **strategy for living fully**.

Warm regards,
Dr. Mandeep Sharma (FIE)
Coach / Mentor / Global Telecom Professional / People Leader / Happiness Advocate

Contents

Part 1:
Mysterious Emotion – Happiness

Chapter 1:
Understanding Happiness

What exactly is happiness for you?

Is it that fleeting joy of a morning coffee? The calm after a long day's work? Or is it something deeper, a steady rhythm of peace, purpose, and fulfilment that quietly anchors our days?

Ask ten different people what happiness means to them, and you will likely hear ten different answers. For some, it's a dream vacation & having a lot of money. For others, it's spending time with loved ones, building something meaningful, or simply waking up without stress. And that's the beauty, and the challenge, of understanding happiness, it is deeply personal, yet universally sought.

For centuries, thinkers from every walk of life, philosophers, poets, saints, and spiritual guides, have reflected on the nature of happiness. They asked, what does it mean to live a good life? Can joy be cultivated, or is it simply a gift of fate? These questions echoed through temples, libraries, and universities alike.

In more recent times, a new set of voices joined the conversation, psychologists, neuroscientists, sociologists, and even economists, offering insights grounded in data, human behaviour, and brain chemistry. And yet, despite the studies and statistics, happiness remains a mystery we're still unfolding, especially in the busy lives of modern professionals.

1.1 Two Faces of Happiness: Hedonic and Eudaimonic

Modern psychology offers us a useful lens to understand happiness through two primary forms, hedonic and eudaimonic.

- **Hedonic happiness** is the kind we're most familiar with, moments of pleasure, comfort, or gratification. Think of enjoying a great meal, receiving praise at work, or watching your favourite show. These moments feel good, but they're often temporary.

- **Eudaimonic happiness**, on the other hand, runs deeper. It is linked to a sense of meaning, growth, and inner alignment. It's not about "feeling good" but about being fulfilled. This kind of happiness is tied to Aristotle's concept of the "good life", a life where we strive not just for ease, but for purpose and excellence.

Busy professionals often find themselves swinging between these two, seeking comfort in small pleasures while longing for something more substantial and sustainable beneath the surface. Real happiness, as emerging science and ancient wisdom agree, comes from balancing both.

Beyond Feel-Good Moments: Flourishing

According to sociologist Corey Keyes, happiness isn't just the absence of sadness or stress, it's a state of positive functioning. In other words, you're not just surviving; you're thriving.

You feel connected. You grow. You contribute.

You have bad days, yes, but they don't define you.

You're not chasing a destination. You're living with direction.

This idea of flourishing is especially relevant for professionals juggling responsibilities, expectations, and the invisible weight of "doing it all." True happiness doesn't ask us to smile all the time, it asks us to live in alignment with what truly matters.

Pause & Reflect

As you step into this journey through the rest of the book, take a moment to ask yourself:

- What does happiness mean to me, right now, at this stage of life?
- Have I been chasing short-term pleasures or nurturing long-term peace?
- Where in my day can I make room for meaning?

Happiness isn't a finish line. It's a direction. And every small, conscious step you take toward it, matters.

Why is it that everyone seems to be chasing happiness, yet so few feel like they have caught it? From early morning alarms to late-night reflections, the pursuit of happiness quietly underlines our daily lives. Whether we admit it or not, much of what we do, working hard, maintaining relationships, making sacrifices, is often motivated by a simple inner hope, "I will be happy once..."

But what does happiness really mean? The truth is, there's no one-size-fits-all answer. For some, happiness means joy and laughter. For others, it's peace and stillness. Some define it as achieving goals; others find it in meaningful connection or a quiet cup of tea after a long day. Despite these personal variations, psychologists often agree on one thing, happiness is best understood as a sustained state of positive emotional well-being, a blend of joy, satisfaction, contentment, and fulfilment.

1.2 Happiness is Both a Feeling and a Lens

When people speak about being happy, they may be describing:

- A momentary state, like feeling joyful after a compliment or a walk in the sun
- Or a broader evaluation of their life, how they feel about their relationships, career, purpose, and health

Because of this dual nature, psychologists often prefer the term "subjective well-being." It's a more precise, personalized way of measuring happiness, not as a momentary mood, but as a deeper sense of how individuals assess the quality of their lives.

Subjective well-being doesn't just reflect temporary highs. It captures how aligned you feel with your values, how connected you are to your community, and how well your life supports your growth.

1.3 Two Key Components of Lasting Happiness

Let's look at two pillars of what experts call subjective well-being:

A. Emotional Balance (The Equilibrium of Feelings)

We all experience both pleasant and unpleasant emotions. That's part of being human. But happiness is strongly associated with having a higher ratio of positive to negative emotions over time. This doesn't mean avoiding sadness or frustration, it means cultivating more moments that uplift you, energize you, and bring warmth to your day. Over time, this emotional balance becomes the foundation of resilience and mental wellness. Imagine a seesaw, happiness doesn't mean removing all the weight from one side, it means gradually adding more lightness to the other.

B. Life Satisfaction

This is the reflective part of happiness. It's when you step back and ask, "Am I living the life I want?" It's about your career, your relationships, your health, your goals, and whether they align with your values and vision. Even when life gets busy or difficult, a high sense of life satisfaction helps you stay grounded, purposeful, and hopeful. It's the compass that reminds you what truly matters.

Real Talk for Busy Professionals

Happiness isn't a destination you reach someday. It's a practice you choose every day.

You don't need to overhaul your life. Sometimes, all it takes is:

- Saying "no" to what drains you
- Saying "yes" to what restores you
- And reminding yourself that you're allowed to feel joy, even when things aren't perfect

1.4 Definitions & the Science of Happiness

"Happiness", it's a word we all use yet often understand differently. Across cultures, disciplines, and generations, happiness has been defined in many ways, as joy, contentment, peace, purpose, and even blessedness. But what are we really referring to when we say we want to be happy?

Broadly, happiness is used in two major contexts:

1. Happiness as an Emotional State (The "Here and Now")

This is the kind of happiness most people talk about casually, the momentary experience of joy, pleasure, or peace. Psychologist and Nobel laureate Daniel Kahneman describes this as "what I experience here and now." It's the feeling of a good laugh, a pleasant walk, or a hug from a loved one. It's real, but often fleeting, what psychologists refer to as affective happiness. These daily emotional highs are valuable. But we all know they don't last. That's why many researchers distinguish it from a second, deeper layer of happiness.

2. Happiness as Life Satisfaction (The Bigger Picture)

This second usage is more reflective, it's about how you evaluate your overall life. Are you living the kind of life you want? Are your values aligned with your daily reality? Sociologist Ruut Veenhoven defines happiness as "the overall appreciation of one's life as a whole." Kahneman, too, observed that while we care about moment-to-moment happiness, we often value long-term satisfaction even more. This duality, emotional experience and life evaluation, is what psychologists call Subjective Well-Being (SWB). It combines how you feel with how you judge your life. As psychologist Sonja Lyubomirsky defines it, "Happiness is the experience of joy, contentment, or positive well-being, combined with a sense that one's life is good, meaningful, and worthwhile."

3. A Third Layer: Eudaimonia – A Flourishing Life

There's another layer that traces back to Greek philosophy, particularly Aristotle's concept of eudaimonia, a state of flourishing, virtue, and living in alignment with one's true self. Here, happiness isn't just about feeling good or evaluating your life, it's about becoming your best self. You grow, you serve, you live with purpose. You flourish. Modern theorists like Xavier Landes expand this idea by integrating eudaimonia, mood, and subjective well-being into a more holistic understanding of happiness.

1.5 Is Happiness Hard-Wired? The Set Point Debate

Some researchers believe we each have a "set point" of happiness, a baseline level shaped by genetics or early experiences. While this theory has some merit, recent research shows we have far more control than once thought. In the words of William James, the "Father of American Psychology", "The greatest discovery of any generation is that human beings can alter their lives by altering their attitudes." Our attitudes, choices, and daily habits shape our happiness more than we often realize.

1.6 The Rise of the Science of Happiness

Until the late 20th century, psychology focused heavily on what's wrong with us, disorders, trauma, breakdowns. But thanks to pioneers like Mihaly Csikszentmihalyi, a new question emerged, What does it mean to truly thrive?

His breakthrough work in the 1980s introduced the **Experience Sampling Method**, which allowed researchers to capture people's emotions and mental states in real-time. This led to the discovery of **Flow**, a state of complete immersion, where challenge meets skill, and time seems to disappear. Flow isn't just about peak performance, it's about deep, personal fulfilment. It's where passion meets purpose.

An Expanding Field: Psychology, Neuroscience & Beyond

Today, the science of happiness spans many disciplines, psychology, sociology, economics, and especially neuroscience, which studies how the brain processes joy, gratitude, and fulfilment. Advanced brain imaging is helping researchers understand how neural circuits respond to positive emotion, and how practices like gratitude, mindfulness, and compassion literally re-wire the brain toward greater well-being. At the same time, positive psychology explores what helps people live thriving lives, not just avoiding illness, but cultivating happiness, meaning, and achievement.

Why This Matters for Busy Professionals

For decades, the field of psychology focused on fixing what's broken. But now, the focus is shifting to helping people rise higher, to live with energy, purpose, and joy. And that shift matters deeply to professionals like you. Because happiness isn't just about what you feel, it's about how you function, lead, create, and connect. What thoughts, habits, and choices make you more fulfilled at the end of the day? Happier in your relationships? More energized at work? The answers aren't abstract, they're practical. That's the promise of the science of happiness.

1.7 The Benefits of Being Happy

Happiness isn't just a pleasant emotion, it's a powerful asset, more so for busy professionals. It fuels resilience during tough times, gives us emotional strength, and encourages a positive outlook. When you're happy, you're not just smiling more, you're equipped to face life's challenges with grace. More than a feel-good state, happiness is a habit, something we can nurture daily. And the benefits of that habit extend well beyond mood. Science now confirms what ancient wisdom has long suggested, happy people live better, fuller, healthier lives.

Here are just a few compelling benefits of being happy:

1. Happiness Improves Physical Health

When you're happy, your body thrives. Research consistently shows that people who report greater happiness experience:

- Fewer hospital visits
- Lower medication usage
- Reduced absenteeism from work
- Healthier cardiovascular profiles

One study found that happier people have a significantly lower risk of dying from heart disease or stroke, even when controlling for weight, exercise, smoking, and alcohol use. Happiness is linked to lower blood pressure, improved cholesterol, and even a reduced risk of heart failure.

Additionally, the findings of the study demonstrated that happiness is associated with reduced blood pressure and healthier cholesterol levels. Moreover, a cheerful disposition may lower the likelihood that you suffer from heart failure.

A 2014 study, which lasted four years and involved nearly a thousand individuals, discovered that high levels of optimism lowered the chance of heart failure by 48%.

So, if you want a healthier heart, a stronger body, and fewer sick days, start by nurturing your happiness.

2. Happiness Boosts Immunity

Your immune system is your first line of defence, and it turns out that your emotional state affects how well it performs. A robust immune system is far more effective at protecting your health and body than a weak one. While a well-balanced diet and healthy lifestyle are crucial, research demonstrates that adopting a joyful and positive way of life can also help boost your immune system.

In one study, 81 healthy graduate students were given the Hepatitis B vaccine. After five months, those who reported higher happiness levels showed nearly double the antibody response compared to less happy peers.

In another trial, 193 individuals were exposed to the common cold virus. Those with more positive emotions were 2.9 times less likely to get sick than those in a negative state.

The takeaway? Happiness doesn't just feel good, it strengthens your body's ability to protect itself. If you want to strengthen your immune system, begin strengthening your happiness first.

3. Happiness Encourages a Healthier Lifestyle

Happy people are more likely to make better lifestyle choices. Studies show they:

- Exercise more regularly
- Eat more fruits and vegetables
- Sleep better
- Are less likely to smoke or abuse substances

A large-scale study involving approximately 10,000 adults found that people who reported higher levels of happiness were more physically active and experienced a slower rate of decline in their level of physical activity.

Another study demonstrated that those who are content are more likely to consume fresh fruits, vegetables, and other nutritious foods.

Happiness reinforces motivation. When you feel good, you want to take care of yourself. And that momentum creates a beautiful cycle of wellness. Your happiness should be your first goal if you want to lead a healthier life.

4. Happiness Reduces Pain

Yes, happiness can reduce physical pain. Happiness doesn't just make you healthier; it also helps you experience less discomfort.

A 2012 study investigated the relationship between positive emotions and knee pain in over 1,000 people suffering from arthritis. Participants who reported greater happiness walked an average of 711 more steps per day, amounting to an 8.5% increase in mobility.

Another study of over 500 individuals with chronic pain showed that happier people reported lower pain levels and were less likely to feel that pain disrupted their daily life. Happiness also triggers endorphins, your brain's natural painkillers.

If you're in discomfort, try to engage in something that brings you joy, it may not cure the pain, but it can make it easier to bear.

5. Happiness May Protect Against Dementia

Happiness supports your brain, too. Dementia is a condition marked by a decline in cognitive function, which can result in memory loss as well as other serious difficulties, particularly for older adults.

A 2021 study published in the Journal of Alzheimer's Disease discovered that individuals who exhibited excessive levels of depressive symptoms in early or late adulthood had a greater likelihood of experiencing cognitive impairment.

Researchers hypothesize that chronic stress and negative emotions may damage the hippocampus, the brain region responsible for memory and learning. Over time, this can accelerate memory loss and decrease mental sharpness.

Want to protect your brain as you age? Protect your peace of mind.

Nurturing emotional well-being today could improve your quality of life in the decades to come.

Final Thoughts on the Benefits

The science is clear, h**appiness is not just a pleasant emotion, it's a health strategy.** It boosts your immunity, reduces pain, protects your heart and brain, and motivates you to make better choices. In short, happy people are not just lucky, they're often healthier, stronger, and more resilient.

And the best part? Happiness can be cultivated, through habits, mindset, purpose, and connection.

1.8 What Really Determines Our Happiness?

What if I told you that a significant part of your happiness isn't about your circumstances, but how you respond to them?

Many people assume that happiness comes from external things, a promotion, a dream home, a vacation, or a relationship. And while these things can absolutely bring moments of joy, research shows they don't determine lasting happiness. So, what does?

Let's explore the three major contributors to long-term happiness, and how much of it is actually in your hands.

1. Genetics (Approx. 50%) – The Set Point Theory

Studies in the field of positive psychology, especially those involving twins, suggest that around 50% of our baseline happiness is determined by genetics. This is often referred to as the "set point."

Just like you might have a natural tendency toward being introverted or extroverted, you may also have a biological predisposition to a more optimistic or pessimistic temperament.

Some people are born with "sunny" emotional wiring. Others may be more prone to anxiety or sadness. But this doesn't mean your emotional destiny is fixed.

Just like fitness or intelligence, happiness can be cultivated, even if your natural baseline is lower.

Think of your genetic set point like your emotional default, but not your emotional ceiling. As psychology professor Sonja Lyubomirsky explains, "It doesn't mean that you're fated to be a certain level of happiness."

2. Life Circumstances (Approx. 10%) – The External Factors

Here's the surprising part, the things most people chase for happiness, wealth, beauty, job title, social status, contribute only about 10% to our overall happiness, according to researcher Sonja Lyubomirsky (whose research is often referred to as the "happiness pie").

That's not to say your environment doesn't matter. Living in poverty, facing discrimination, or being in a toxic workplace can understandably diminish well-being. But for most people in reasonably stable situations, life circumstances have less influence than we think.

Why? Because we adapt. This is called hedonic adaptation, our tendency to return to a baseline level of happiness even after major positive or negative events.

You get a raise, you're thrilled. A few months later, it's just your new normal. You move to a better house, it feels amazing. Then, life returns to routine.

We quickly get used to "better," and it no longer boosts our mood long-term.

3. Intentional Activities (Approx. 40%) – Your Daily Choices

Here's the game-changer, up to 40% of your happiness is within your voluntary control. This means your thoughts, behaviours, habits, and mindset play a much bigger role than your circumstances. It's not about pretending everything is perfect, but learning how to create meaning, joy, and resilience within what you already have.

Intentional activities include:

- Practicing **gratitude**
- Nurturing **positive relationships**
- Engaging in **purposeful work**
- Prioritizing **rest and recovery**
- Committing to **personal growth**
- Investing in **moments of joy** and play
- Reframing challenges with a **growth mindset**

As simple as these practices may sound, they have a compounding effect. Just like daily exercise builds physical strength, daily happiness habits build emotional strength.

Happiness Formula from Credible Experts

To further illustrate these concepts, here are some recognized happiness formulae from credible experts:

1. The "Set Point Theory" Formula – Sonja Lyubomirsky et al.

   Happiness = Set Point (50%) + Life Circumstances (10%) + Intentional Activities (40%)

   This model highlights that 50% of our happiness is genetically determined, 10% is influenced by life circumstances, and 40% is within our voluntary control through mindset, habits, and intentional choices.

2. The PERMA Model – Dr. Martin Seligman

   Happiness = P + E + R + M + A

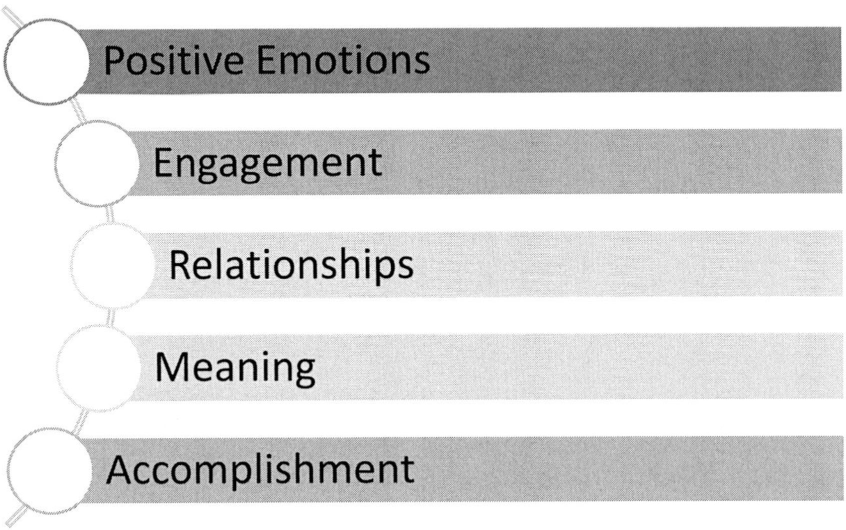

   This model is central to Positive Psychology and is used globally in well-being programs.

3. The Japanese "Ikigai" Formula

   Ikigai = What You Love + What You're Good At + What the World Needs + What You Can Be Paid For

   This model represents aligning life with purpose to create happiness and vitality.

4. The Happiness Equation – Neil Pasricha

   Happiness = Want Nothing + Do Anything = Have Everything

   A mindset formula that emphasizes detachment, purpose-driven action, and gratitude.

5. Mandeep's Signature Happiness Formula

   Happiness = A × (M + E + R + S)

Where:

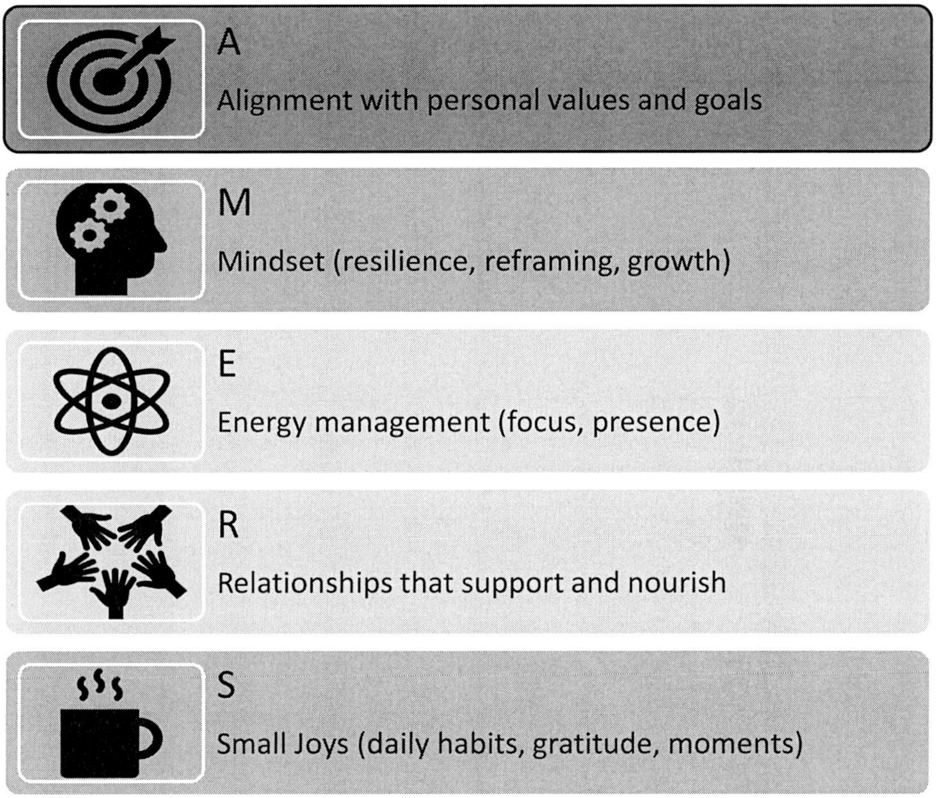

This practical formula fits the complex lives of busy professionals and can be visualized through the Happiness Compass metaphor.

The Power of Neuroplasticity & Happiness

Modern neuroscience supports this idea. Through **neuroplasticity**, your brain can rewire itself based on what you focus on and how you behave. Repeatedly practicing gratitude can strengthen pathways associated with positivity. Mindfulness and meditation can shrink the fear centres of your brain. Acts of kindness light up reward circuits more than receiving rewards. You're not stuck with the brain you were born with. You're shaping it, every day.

Coaching Reflection: Take the Driver's Seat

As a coach and mentor, I often ask my colleagues & professionals, "If 40% of your happiness is in your control, what are you doing with it today?"

The answer doesn't have to be grand. It can be as small as, calling a friend instead of scrolling your phone, writing down 3 things you're grateful for, saying "no" to one obligation that drains you, or doing something that feels playful, not productive. It's not about being happy all the time. It's about cultivating happiness over time, through consistent, aligned actions.

In summary, happiness is not an accident. It's a skill. A practice. A mindset.

And while you can't always control what happens around you, you can always influence what happens within you.

Key Learnings

- Around **40% of your happiness is within your daily control**.
- **Intentional habits** like gratitude, connection, and purpose have lasting impact.
- **Adaptation** makes external achievements short-lived; inner growth sustains happiness.

Quick Actionables

- Start a **3-minute gratitude journal** every morning.
- Choose one "**small joy**" to prioritize daily, something just for you.
- Reflect on one **thought pattern** you can reframe this week.

1.9 Habits that Build Lasting Happiness

If happiness isn't something we stumble upon, but something we cultivate, then our daily habits are the soil in which it grows.

For professionals like us, caught between deadlines and decisions, it's easy to think we need a massive transformation to feel better. But the truth is simpler, and far more hopeful, **small daily habits can change the entire tone of your life.**

We don't need to overhaul everything. We just need to start intentionally, and build gradually. Let's explore the habits that research and experience both tell us have the greatest impact on long-term happiness.

1. Gratitude: The Foundation of Fulfilment

Gratitude is not just saying "thank you", it's training your mind to notice what's already good.

Studies show that people who practice gratitude:

- Sleep better
- Experience fewer symptoms of depression
- Have stronger immune systems
- Build better relationships

Start simple:

- Each morning, write down **three things you're thankful for.**
- Make it specific: *"The quiet moment with my tea before emails"* is more powerful than *"my job."*
- Say thank you to different people every day, personally, genuinely, even silently in your mind.

Gratitude turns ordinary moments into blessings.

2. Acts of Kindness: The Happiness Multiplier

When we help others, we often feel a "helper's high", a surge of serotonin and oxytocin. It turns out, kindness isn't selfless, it's mutually uplifting.

Research shows that people who perform regular acts of kindness:

- Report greater overall life satisfaction
- Experience fewer negative emotions
- Build deeper social bonds

Try this:

- Compliment a colleague sincerely
- Help someone without being asked

- Send a message to someone who needs encouragement

These tiny actions compound, and you will start to feel not just useful, but connected.

3. Mindfulness: Training the Mind to Be Present

We often replay the past or worry about the future, while the only place happiness can exist is now. Mindfulness means gently bringing your attention to the present moment, without judgment. Just noticing.

- Through meditation
- While eating slowly
- By taking a 2-minute breathing break between meetings

Busy schedule? No problem. Start with just one breath of awareness. That's mindfulness in action.

Presence is power. And mindfulness is the doorway to it.

4. Strengthening Relationships: Connection is the Cornerstone

The longest-running study on happiness, conducted by Harvard over 80+ years, found one clear truth, "Good relationships keep us happier and healthier. Period."

Not money. Not fame. Not status.

Strong, supportive relationships, whether with a partner, a close friend, or a mentor, are the single most consistent predictor of well-being.

Simple ways to strengthen connections:

- Put your phone away during meals
- Make time to call a friend once a week
- Express appreciation regularly

When we feel seen and heard, happiness takes root.

5. Creating Meaning: Live with Intentional Goals

Many people confuse happiness with pleasure. But lasting happiness often comes from meaning, doing something that matters.

You don't need to change careers. Just ask:

- *What gives me a sense of purpose?*
- *When do I feel most energized and useful?*

Whether it's mentoring someone, volunteering, building a side project, or raising a family with care, purpose deepens joy. Set small, purposeful goals and celebrate progress, not perfection. Enjoy the journey!

6. Letting Go of Comparison and Embracing Self-Compassion

In a world filled with highlight reels, comparing yourself to others is a shortcut to unhappiness. Instead, practice self-compassion, treating yourself with the same kindness you'd offer a friend. Try this, Catch your inner critic, "I failed again" → "I'm learning and trying." Write yourself a note of encouragement. Acknowledge effort, not just outcomes. You are not behind, you're on your own path. And you deserve kindness from yourself most of all.

7. The Compound Effect of Joyful Habits

None of these habits need to be done perfectly. What matters is consistency. Happiness isn't built in grand gestures. It's built in, the morning you journaled instead of scrolled, the moment you paused and breathed before reacting, and the walk you took without your phone. Each action is like depositing a coin into your emotional savings account. Over time, the balance grows.

Coaching Note: Design Your Habit Stack

If you're overwhelmed, start with one. Attach it to something you already do. For example, after brushing your teeth → write 3 gratitudes; After your first meeting → take 3 deep breaths; While your coffee brews → send a kind message. This technique is called **habit stacking**, and it works beautifully for professionals with packed schedules.

Key Learnings

- **Daily habits**, not big events, create sustainable happiness.
- Gratitude, kindness, mindfulness, and connection are powerful happiness multipliers.
- Small, intentional actions done consistently lead to compounding emotional wellbeing.

Quick Actionables

- Start a **3-minute gratitude ritual** every morning.
- Do one **kind thing** daily, without expecting anything in return.
- Replace your scroll break with a **2-minute breathing pause**.
- Call or message **one person today** who makes you feel connected.

1.10 The Myths That Block Our Happiness

We all want to be happy. We chase goals, earn accolades, and upgrade our lifestyles, hoping happiness will follow. But what if one of the biggest reasons we feel emotionally unfulfilled isn't because of what we're missing, but because of what we have misunderstood? It's not the stress. It's not the workload. It's not the circumstances. It's the unseen myths we have inherited about what happiness is "supposed" to be.

These myths silently shape our expectations. They whisper false promises. And worst of all, they make us question ourselves when we don't feel the way we think we should.

Let's shine a light on these myths, unpack them one by one, and release ourselves from them, gently, with awareness.

Myth 1: "Success Will Make Me Happy"

This one is a classic, "Once I get that promotion, once I buy the house, once I achieve this milestone, then I will finally be happy." It sounds logical. But it rarely works that way.

Success brings temporary joy, but not lasting happiness. This is duc to something psychologists call the hedonic treadmill, we get used to the new achievement, and our happiness baseline resets. We begin chasing the next milestone. And the next.

Coaching Reframe: What if success wasn't the goal but the result? Studies show happier people are more productive, creative, and resilient. So instead of waiting for success to bring happiness, invest in happiness to fuel sustainable success.

Truth: Happiness fuels success, not the other way around.

Quick Actionable: Reflect on a recent success. Did it bring lasting happiness, or did you quickly shift focus to the next thing? Celebrate your wins with presence, not pressure.

Myth 2: "Money Will Make You Happy"

Money absolutely matters, especially when it comes to meeting basic needs and feeling secure. But beyond a certain point, more money doesn't equal more happiness.

A Princeton University study in 2010 by Nobel laureates Daniel Kahneman and Angus Deaton showed that if your fundamental requirements are satisfied, your degree of happiness reaches a plateau, which normally occurs at income levels of $75,000 or more per year.

However, in 2021, research conducted by Matthew Killingsworth at the University of Pennsylvania disputed these findings, showing that greater salaries did improve happiness without reaching a plateau. To reconcile these contrasting results, researchers from both camps joined in an "adversarial collaboration" in a 2023 study.

Their findings concluded that income can continue to enhance happiness, but only for those who are already happy. For those who are unhappy, more money does not significantly change emotional well-being.

As Killingsworth puts it in an article in Penn Today, “Money is not the secret to happiness, but it can probably help a bit.”

Coaching Reframe: Ask yourself, is money buying me time, freedom, or experiences, or just more things?

Truth: Money supports happiness, but it doesn’t define it.

Quick Actionable: Make one small decision today to prioritize time or connection over money, like spending an hour with someone you love instead of chasing one more task.

Myth 3: "Material Things Will Make You Happy"

Retail therapy feels good, for a moment. But that new phone, bag, or car quickly becomes the new normal. The joy fades. You’re left with clutter and a craving for the next fix. This is a phenomenon known as hedonic adaptation. As psychologist Sophia Godkin states, "Investing in material possessions offers a certain degree of initial satisfaction. However, that satisfaction and happiness began to decrease not long after." She also notes that people engage in social comparisons, "All of a sudden, I'm no longer as happy as I was," when they notice someone else has a newer, more expensive version.

Science says, we adapt quickly to things, but we savour experiences. Vacations, meaningful conversations, time in nature, these moments leave emotional imprints.

On the other hand, research has shown that more materialistic persons tend to have lower levels of happiness compared to their peers. "They experience fewer positive emotions, are less satisfied with life, and suffer higher levels of anxiety, depression, and substance abuse," states the Greater Good Science Centre in Berkeley, California.

Truth: Joy lives in moments, not possessions.

Quick Actionable: Instead of buying something today, plan an experience, invite a friend to coffee, take a walk, or create something.

Myth 4: "I Should Always Feel Positive"

This myth is dangerous because it invalidates our real human experience. Life comes with stress, sorrow, confusion. That doesn't mean we're failing at happiness. Emotional honesty is foundational to well-being. Ignoring emotions creates emotional pressure and shame.

Truth: Happiness is not constant cheerfulness. It's about being whole, not perfect.

Quick Actionable: Give yourself permission today to feel. No filters. No fixes. Just awareness.

Myth 5: "Others Have It Better"

In the age of Instagram, comparison is inevitable. But remember, what people show is not what they live. Comparison robs us of joy. Connection restores it.

Truth: Everyone has their own silent struggles. The only life you need to live fully is your own.

Quick Actionable: Unfollow three accounts that make you feel less-than. Follow one that makes you feel inspired and grounded.

Myth 6: "I Don't Have Time to Be Happy"

You don't need hours of meditation or weekend retreats. You need intention in the moment. Small actions like a 3-minute breath, a gratitude note, or stepping outside for sunlight can reset your nervous system and re-centre your mind.

Truth: Happiness doesn't need more time, it needs more awareness.

Quick Actionable: Block just five minutes today for something that brings you peace. Schedule it like a meeting.

Myth 7: "Happiness Means Always Smiling"

Smiling is great, but it isn't the full picture. Real happiness allows space for boundaries, silence, and authenticity. Sometimes, the happiest thing you can do is take a break, say no, or cry.

Truth: You don't have to smile to be okay. Being real is being well.

Quick Actionable: Practice one act of authenticity today, even if it's just saying, "I'm not okay right now, but I will be."

Myth 8: "Being Happy Means Being Selfish"

This myth is deeply ingrained, especially in caregivers, professionals, and parents. We equate self-sacrifice with worth. But you can't pour from an empty cup. When you're well, everyone around you benefits.

Truth: Self-care is not indulgence, it's leadership.

Quick Actionable: Do one small thing for yourself today, guilt-free. That's not luxury. That's self-respect.

Myth 9: "I Can Control Everything"

The more we cling to control, the more stressed we feel. Happiness comes not from controlling outcomes but from choosing responses.

Truth: Let go. Flow with change. Anchor in values, not variables.

Quick Actionable: Write down three things today you can control, and three you can release.

Myth 10: "My Past Defines My Future"

Yes, your past has shaped you. But it does not own you. Thanks to neuroplasticity, your brain can form new patterns. New thoughts. New outcomes.

Truth: Your story is still unfolding. And you hold the pen.

Quick Actionable: Write a new narrative. One sentence. One affirmation. One belief to carry forward.

Myth 11: "If I'm Not Happy, Something is Wrong with Me"

Some days are heavy. That's not failure. That's being human.

Chasing constant happiness creates anxiety. Instead, aim for presence, meaning, and grace.

Truth: Fluctuation is normal. Feelings are messengers, not enemies.

Quick Actionable: Instead of fixing your mood today, sit with it. Ask: What is this feeling asking from me?

Myth 12: "Happiness is Genetic"

Genes play a role, but they're not the whole story. About 40% of your happiness is under your intentional control. Habits like gratitude, movement, kindness, and reframing thoughts change your brain's chemistry over time.

Truth: Happiness is a skill. Practice makes peace.

Quick Actionable: Pick one new happiness habit this week and stick with it for 7 days.

Myth 13: "Losing Weight Will Make You Happy"

Weight loss might affect confidence, but true happiness comes from self-respect, purpose, and emotional health. Focusing solely on appearance often leads to frustration and shame.

Truth: You deserve joy, now, not when you look different.

Quick Actionable: Thank your body today, for carrying you, supporting you, healing you.

Myth 14: "If You Become Disabled, You will Never Be Happy Again"

This myth is deeply unfair. Many individuals living with disabilities report high levels of life satisfaction. Why? Because happiness isn't dependent on physical perfection, it's rooted in purpose, community, and mindset.

Truth: Happiness is possible in every body, every season, every story.

Quick Actionable: Watch or read a story about someone thriving despite adversity. Let it inspire, not compare.

Coaching Reflection: Rewrite One Myth

Pick the myth that hit home the most.

- Write it down.
- Then write your new truth.

Old Belief: I will be happy when I achieve more.

New Truth: I can choose joy in the process, not just the outcome.

Small rewrites create big shifts.

Key Learnings

- Our happiness is often blocked not by life, but by unchallenged beliefs.
- Many happiness myths come from outdated cultural, social, or emotional programming.
- Rewriting our internal scripts creates space for real, grounded joy.

Quick Actionables

- Identify one happiness myth you have been living, rewrite it.
- Share a reframe with a friend or loved one.
- Say out loud each morning: "My happiness is mine to create."

Let go of the myths. Embrace the truth. Happiness begins there.

References:

1. https://www.ncbi.nlm.nih.gov/pmc/articles/PMC4040132/
2. https://pubmed.ncbi.nlm.nih.gov/15321995/
3. https://pubmed.ncbi.nlm.nih.gov/12672894/
4. https://pubmed.ncbi.nlm.nih.gov/22589238/
5. https://content.iospress.com/articles/journal-of-alzheimers-disease/jad210428

Sources:

1. Lyubomirsky, Sheldon, & Schkade (2005) – 'Pursuing Happiness: The Architecture of Sustainable Change'.
2. Martin Seligman – 'Flourish' (2011).
3. Héctor García & Francesc Miralles – 'Ikigai' (2016).
4. Neil Pasricha – 'The Happiness Equation' (2016)

Chapter 2:
The Pursuit of Happiness

2.1 The Pursuit of Happiness: West Meets East

The phrase "the pursuit of happiness" has often been profoundly misunderstood. It was never meant to endorse an endless, material chase for fleeting pleasures or external wealth. Instead, its true intent was far deeper: it referred to the pursuit of a **meaningful life**, a life where one's actions are infused with purpose, where each day feels inherently worth living, and where personal well-being is intentionally cultivated.

The modern understanding of happiness in the West places **personal freedom** at its very foundation. It is believed that only when individuals are free, free to think, choose, and act autonomously, can they truly align with their inner calling. This belief is powerfully captured by psychologist James Hillman in what he called "the soul's code." According to Hillman, each of us carries within a unique blueprint, a code of destiny that cannot be dictated by parents, society, or even circumstance. Fulfillment, then, is not manufactured externally but discovered internally. Happiness, in this view, is about **alignment, not accumulation.**

This idea was central to the founding of the United States. The Declaration of Independence boldly asserted each person's inalienable right to "life, liberty, and the pursuit of happiness." Crucially, this didn't promise happiness itself, it promised the freedom to pursue it. The intent was to create the conditions where happiness could genuinely flourish: **personal autonomy, individual choice, and the ability to follow one's own unique life path.** This principle sharply contrasts with the ideals of the French Revolution, liberté, égalité, fraternité, which emphasized collective societal values. While both traditions aimed to enhance human dignity, America leaned into individual agency, whereas France leaned into shared identity.

Napoleon's vision later embedded these collectivist ideals across Europe, creating a cultural divergence that continues today: one that values inner freedom versus one that prioritizes societal equity. The Founding Fathers didn't equate happiness with material wealth. They believed in the benefits of a free-market economy, but not as an end in itself. Wealth was a tool, not a destination. What mattered more was the freedom to create, innovate, and live a meaningful life. Even the economic policies of the early American revolution were rooted in the desire to escape British restrictions that stifled personal and economic expression.

Now, let's journey Eastward.

Eastern Wisdom: Inner Harmony as the Foundation of Joy

While the West spoke of the "pursuit" of happiness, Eastern philosophies, especially Indian thought, spoke of **realizing** it. In ancient texts like the Bhagavad Gita, Upanishads, and Buddhist teachings, happiness is seen not as something to chase endlessly but as something **already present**, inherent in our true nature, merely veiled by ignorance, ego, and craving.

In the Gita, Lord Krishna reminds Arjuna that true contentment arises from **Dharma**, living in alignment with one's duty and values, without attachment to results. In this wisdom, happiness comes not from outcomes, but from purposeful, mindful action rooted in one's soul. The Upanishads teach that the **Self (Atman) is bliss**. The more we truly know ourselves, not just intellectually, but spiritually, the more profound peace and joy we uncover. It's not about what we have, but about who we become. Buddhism, too, offers a rich view: happiness is **freedom from suffering** achieved through transcending desires and attachments. Through the Noble Eightfold Path, right thought, right action, right livelihood, etc., one cultivates inner equanimity, mindfulness, and compassion. These aren't lofty ideals. They are daily disciplines that can be woven into the fabric of even the busiest professional's life.

And in modern times, Bhutan introduced the world to **Gross National Happiness (GNH)**, a framework that measures national progress not by GDP, but by the collective well-being of its citizens. GNH includes psychological wellness, community vitality, environmental conservation, and cultural preservation, offering a holistic, human-centered model of progress that the world increasingly looks to with respect.

Bridging the Two Worlds

Whether from the East or West, the core message is strikingly similar: true happiness is not a product of accumulation but of **alignment**. It is about living in sync with your deeper self, your values, your purpose, your relationships, and your core energy.

In the West, we speak of freedom to choose. In the East, we speak of freedom from illusion. Together, they create a fuller, more profound picture. **The pursuit of happiness is about finding genuine fulfillment, not just fleeting pleasure.** It means honoring your authentic self, engaging with the world mindfully, and cultivating inner peace amidst external demands.

As busy professionals, this distinction matters deeply. We live in high-speed environments with endless demands, often driven by external metrics of success. But the pursuit of happiness does not require escaping to the Himalayas or quitting your job. It requires **coming home to what truly matters, within.** Happiness is not found in comparison, consumption, or external control. It's found in **clarity, authentic connection, compassion, and the courage to live life authentically, on your own terms.**

Key Learnings:

- **Happiness is Found in Alignment, Not Accumulation:** Both Western and Eastern traditions converge on this truth: happiness is not about material wealth or fleeting pleasures but about living in harmony with one's deeper purpose and values. Alignment with your soul's code, or Dharma, matters more than external success.
- **Freedom is the Foundation of Fulfillment:** In the Western view, especially in the American founding philosophy, personal freedom is seen as a precondition for pursuing happiness. This mirrors Eastern teachings that emphasize inner liberation, freedom from ego, attachment, and societal conditioning. **True freedom is both external liberty and internal peace.**
- **Your Path is Unique, And Inwardly Guided:** Drawing from James Hillman's "soul's code" and the Indian idea of *Swadharma* (one's unique duty), true happiness comes from within, guided by an inner compass rather than external expectations. **Your happiness journey is deeply personal and unfolds from within.**
- **Collective and Personal Well-Being Are Interconnected:** While Western thought emphasizes the individual's right to pursue happiness, Eastern traditions emphasize interconnectedness (*Vasudhaiva Kutumbakam*, the world is one family). True happiness considers both personal fulfillment and collective harmony. **Our well-being is linked to the well-being of others.**
- **The Pursuit of Happiness Is a Lifelong Inner Journey:** The Declaration of Independence promises the "pursuit" of happiness, not a guaranteed state. Similarly, in Eastern philosophy, happiness is seen as an evolving journey, cultivated through mindfulness, balance, and spiritual growth. **It's a continuous process of self-discovery and conscious living.**

Quick Actionable:

- **Clarify Your Inner Compass:** Take 15 minutes weekly to reflect: "What truly matters to me? What gives my life meaning beyond my job title?" This helps align your daily decisions with your deeper purpose, not external validation.
- **Write Your Personal Declaration:** Just like the U.S. Declaration, write your own 3-point version: My values. My purpose. My definition of happiness. Acts as your personal mission statement to anchor you amidst professional busyness.
- **Practice 5-Minute Inner Freedom:** Daily pause to release mental clutter. Breathe and say: "In this moment, I choose peace over pressure." Brings Eastern mindfulness into Western productivity, centering you in freedom.
- **Reconnect with Your Dharma (Personal Role):** Ask yourself: Am I living by others' expectations or my own calling? Adjust 1 task this week to reflect your authentic values. Rooted in Eastern wisdom, reconnects you with *Swadharma*, your unique path.
- **Blend Self & Society:** Identify 1 action this week that benefits both you and someone else (e.g., mentoring, volunteering, team support). Brings balance between Western individualism and Eastern interdependence.
- **Reset Your Definition of Success:** Redefine success not as "more," but as "more aligned." Review your goals, what would feel authentic, not just impressive? Helps break the trap of accumulation and align with meaning.

2.2 The Factors that Contribute to Happiness

Happiness isn't a one-size-fits-all concept. It is shaped by a wide array of internal and external influences, some within our control, and others beyond it. Understanding these factors empowers us to cultivate more joy intentionally, while also fostering acceptance for what cannot be changed. Each person experiences happiness in their own way. Some seem naturally more joyful, interpreting life's events with optimism and resilience. But beyond temperament, research shows that happiness is influenced by a mix of genetic, environmental, psychological, and lifestyle elements.

Happiness isn't a random stroke of luck. It's a complex, evolving blend of factors that include our biology, our environment, our mindset, and the quality of our choices and relationships. Some of these elements are within our control, while others are shaped by our circumstances or even our DNA. But here's the empowering truth: even when we cannot control a factor, we can choose how we respond to it. That's where our greatest power lies.

As a coach, I have often seen people chase happiness in external achievements, only to discover that the answers lie much closer to home. In this section, we will dive deep into each key contributor to happiness, what the science says, what real life reflects, and how you, as a busy professional, can actively cultivate more of it.

1. Genetic Predisposition

What It Means: Scientific studies suggest that approximately 40% to 50% of a person's baseline happiness is influenced by their genetic makeup. Researchers like Sonja Lyubomirsky and David Lykken, in twin studies, found that people seem to have a "set point" for happiness, like a thermostat, that they tend to return to even after major life events.

Coaching Reflection: You may know someone who always seems upbeat, no matter what. That's temperament, and yes, part of it is inherited. But don't mistake this for destiny. Genetics set the stage, but you get to direct the play.

Example: Consider two professionals receiving the same disappointing feedback at work. One shrugs it off, using it as motivation; the other spirals into anxiety. Genetics may explain the initial emotional response, but habits, mindset, and emotional tools determine how each moves forward.

Actionable:

- Don't compare your emotional baseline to others'. Instead, track your own emotional patterns.
- Create a 7-day "Happiness Log" to note moments of joy and gratitude, helping shift your internal set point over time.

2. Physical Health

What It Means: Numerous studies confirm the powerful link between physical health and emotional well-being. Exercise triggers endorphins, sleep regulates mood, and good nutrition supports brain chemistry. According to Harvard Health, even moderate aerobic activity can reduce symptoms of anxiety and depression.

Coaching Reflection: As busy professionals, we often treat health as an afterthought, until it becomes the main thought. But your energy, mood, and motivation are directly tied to how you treat your body.

Example: A senior executive once shared with me that simply switching to 20-minute morning walks dramatically improved both his mood and his team's morale. Why? Because his energy shifted, and so did the culture he influenced.

Actionable:

- Move your body at least 20 minutes daily. Walking counts.
- Improve one meal per day by adding whole, colorful foods.
- Create a "Digital Sunset" where you turn off screens 1 hour before bed.

3. Quality of Relationships

What It Means: The Harvard Study of Adult Development, one of the longest studies ever conducted, found that the strongest predictor of long-term happiness and health is not wealth, fame, or success, but quality relationships. Love, connection, and community keep us emotionally grounded.

Coaching Reflection: When people come to me feeling stuck, the root often lies in emotional isolation. Connection is not a luxury, it's a psychological necessity.

Example: During one of my group coaching sessions, a high-performing client admitted she hadn't had a heartfelt conversation in months. Her "happiness reboot" started with one dinner with an old friend. That evening did more than 50 webinars could.

Actionable:

- Reconnect with one person this week with a short call or coffee.
- Express genuine appreciation to someone in your life, right now.
- Schedule a recurring "connection hour" weekly with a loved one.

4. Work Life

What It Means: Our careers consume a significant portion of our waking lives. Work that feels meaningful, aligned, and autonomous enhances happiness. A 2022 Gallup study found that employee engagement, not salary, was the strongest predictor of happiness at work.

Coaching Reflection: Many professionals I coach are deeply successful, on paper. But behind closed doors, they feel trapped, exhausted, or invisible. The truth is: it's not about working less. It's about working where you feel seen, valued, and trusted.

Example: A mid-level manager in my office in Mumbai once told me, "I used to hate Mondays until I realized it wasn't the work, it was the lack of recognition." He started a weekly peer-appreciation ritual on his team. It changed the atmosphere, and he found renewed energy.

Actionable:

- Reflect: Does your work align with your core values? List 3 ways it does, or doesn't.
- If misaligned, start small: redesign your current role to include what energizes you.
- Appreciate a colleague each week, positive work cultures begin with one person.

5. Money and Financial Attitude

What It Means: Money affects happiness, but mostly in its ability to remove stress. Studies, including research from Princeton in USA, suggest that after a certain threshold (around $75,000–$90,000 annual income), additional money contributes little to day-to-day emotional well-being. Beyond that point, perception and financial security matter more than income level.

Coaching Reflection: We're conditioned to believe more is better. But happiness doesn't come from how much you earn, it comes from whether your lifestyle and values are aligned. Wealth without peace is just a gilded cage.

Example: One of my highly accomplished customer in Mumbai downsized from a luxury condo to a simpler home in Navi Mumbai. The result? More savings, less stress, and deeper joy from spending weekends cycling, instead of managing a high-maintenance lifestyle. He said, "I finally bought my freedom back."

Actionable:

- Track what brings real joy: Is it spending, or peace of mind?
- Build a 3-month emergency fund, it's not just security, it's emotional leverage.
- Practice mindful spending: ask "Will this enhance my happiness or clutter it?"

6. Attitude and Mindset

What It Means: How we interpret events shapes our emotional reality. Psychologist Martin Seligman's work in positive psychology shows that learned optimism, the ability to interpret setbacks as temporary and changeable, leads to greater resilience and happiness.

Coaching Reflection: Your mind is not a mirror. It's a lens. The way you explain events to yourself creates either empowerment or despair. The good news? That lens can be trained.

Example: During a coaching session, a participant shared that after losing a major customer, she began repeating, "This is a redirection, not a rejection." Within weeks, she found an even better-fit partnership. Her mindset transformed her momentum.

Actionable:

- When facing a setback, reframe: "What is this teaching me?"
- Also start a "Victory Journal": Write down 3 small wins daily to train your focus on the positive.
- Limit exposure to negative news and environments that drain optimism.

7. Sense of Control and Autonomy

What It Means: People who believe they have control over their lives experience significantly higher levels of happiness. According to Deci and Ryan's Self-Determination Theory, autonomy, the ability to choose one's actions, is a fundamental psychological need. Feeling "stuck" or powerless erodes emotional well-being.

Coaching Reflection: If you often feel like life is "happening to you," you're not alone. But every decision, no matter how small, can be a vote toward reclaiming your power. Even choosing how you respond is a form of autonomy.

Example: One coachee, overwhelmed in a high-pressure leadership role, started each day by simply choosing her top 3 priorities instead of reacting to her overflowing inbox. That one choice gave her back her time, and her sense of command.

Actionable:

- Identify one area in your life where you feel disempowered. What's one micro-decision you can reclaim today?
- Create a "Choice Audit", list decisions you've deferred to others, and ask: which ones can I own again?
- Practice saying no to things that don't serve your goals. Every no to others is a yes to yourself.

8. Personal Values

What It Means: Personal values are your inner compass, guiding your decisions, shaping your goals, and anchoring your identity. Research shows that living in alignment with your values increases life satisfaction, reduces regret, and builds resilience in adversity.

Coaching Reflection: When you feel lost, misaligned, or empty despite success, it's usually a sign you've drifted from your values. Realignment brings peace, not because life is perfect, but because it finally makes sense.

Example: A tech consultant once told me, "I feel like I'm succeeding in a life I didn't sign up for." We explored his values, and he rediscovered his love for mentoring. He shifted his role slightly and now leads a leadership development program. Same job. Different fuel.

Actionable:

- Write your top 5 core values. (e.g., honesty, creativity, service, family, growth)
- Review your calendar and bank statement. Are you living in alignment with what you claim to value?
- Choose one daily action, however small, that reflects one of your top values.

9. Success and Balance

What It Means: Success and happiness can be mutually reinforcing, but they're not the same. True success is meaningful, self-defined, and sustainable. When we chase titles or wealth without purpose, happiness becomes a casualty. When success reflects values and joy, it becomes fuel.

Coaching Reflection: I often ask my clients: "Who defined your version of success?" If the answer isn't you, it's time to revise the script. A busy life can be successful, but only a balanced one can be joyful.

Example: A senior VP once shared, "I used to feel guilty for taking Sundays off." After we explored the costs of burnout, she began protecting her weekends like gold. Her performance improved, but more importantly, so did her peace.

Actionable:

- Redefine success: What does it feel like, not just look like?
- Do a "Joy vs. Achievement" audit of your current goals. Are they aligned?
- Schedule one sacred block per week for your well-being, and treat it like a boardroom meeting.

Chapter Key Learnings

- Happiness is not a fixed state—it's an evolving practice influenced by health, mindset, work, and relationships.
- Personal agency, value alignment, and authentic success matter more than external markers.
- Strong relationships, meaningful work, and autonomy form the emotional core of well-being.

Quick Actionables

- Start a 7-day Happiness Journal to reflect on your daily triggers and emotional patterns.
- Audit your life for alignment with your top 5 values. Adjust one habit accordingly.
- Choose one area where you feel disempowered—and take a micro-action to reclaim it.
- Reach out to a trusted friend or colleague this week and schedule intentional connection.

Quick Happiness Hacks – For Busy Professionals

Frequency	Actionable	Theme
Daily	Start your day with 2 minutes of deep breathing or mindfulness before checking your phone.	De-stress & Mindfulness
Daily	Journal one thing you're grateful for and one thing you're looking forward to.	Gratitude & Reflection
Daily	Take a 10-minute walk outdoors during lunch to reset and re-energize.	Connecting to Nature
Daily	Speak one kind sentence to yourself when faced with stress or self-doubt.	Self-Compassion
Daily	Drink water mindfully, hydrate as a small act of self-care.	Well-being & Health
Weekly	Have a 'tech-free' hour in the evening to recharge emotionally.	Digital Detox
Weekly	Schedule a 1-on-1 coffee or call with a friend or mentor to stay connected.	Relationships & Connection
Weekly	Reflect on your energy levels at week's end and plan 1 joyful activity for next week.	Joyful Planning
Weekly	Do a weekly review of tasks done vs. what brought meaning or fulfillment.	Core Values & Fulfillment
Weekly	Volunteer or offer help to someone in your network without expecting anything in return.	Contribution & Service
Monthly	Review your long-term goals: Are you aligned with what truly matters to you?	Core Values & Life Goals
Monthly	Unplug for a half-day and immerse in a passion project or nature outing.	Nature & Passion Projects
Monthly	Declutter one part of your home or workspace that causes visual or emotional stress.	Emotional Clarity
Monthly	Book time in your calendar for a personal retreat day (rest, reflect, reset).	Self-Renewal

Chapter 3:
Mindset and Happiness

3.1 The Mindset Map – How Your Thinking Shapes Your Happiness

Happiness, at its core, is entirely a matter of perspective. Contrary to popular assumption, internal elements such as perception, mindset, and belief system often have a greater influence on our happiness than do external factors.

Does it seem overly philosophical?

Let's break it down: you probably know people who appear genuinely happy and content with their lives, despite not owning the most expensive cars, having an extensive designer wardrobe, or excessive wealth. On the other hand, even though they may appear to have everything going well for them, many people in the world seem unhappy and depressed.

In an interview, Michelle Obama powerfully asserted, "Barack and the kids add to my happiness. They have no say over it; I decide what makes me happy and I decide to be happy." She is essentially asserting control over her own emotional state and refusing to let outside forces dictate it. Her insights emphasize that happiness is a personal choice, and your thinking profoundly determines how happy you are.

Life will always have setbacks. Nobody is immune to difficulties or issues; even saints or monks cannot escape them. But these challenges can be addressed head-on when they emerge, allowing you to relish the happy times in life. You reclaim your power over happiness when you develop an attitude that remains undisturbed by external turbulence. As the Greek philosopher Aristotle stated, happiness is "the meaning and the purpose of life; the whole aim and end of human existence."

Regaining our autonomy in life can be facilitated by adopting a mindset that accepts happiness; it gives us the power to choose joy. If you are constantly looking outside of yourself for happiness, in the form of money, social groups, or achievements, you are likely trying to fill an endless well, because nothing external will ever be fully adequate. This reflects the **Law of Diminishing Returns**, which asserts that the more we experience something, the less gratifying it becomes over time.

What then is this "mindset"?

Have you ever noticed how two people can go through the exact same situation, and walk away with completely different reactions?

One sees an obstacle; the other sees an opportunity.

One dwells in frustration; the other moves forward with hope.

The difference? It's not the situation. It's the mindset.

Mindset is the mental lens through which we experience the world. It shapes our interpretation of events, our emotional responses, and even our sense of self-worth. Think of it as the *mental software* running in the background, quietly influencing how we perceive our past, act in the present, and anticipate the future.

The term *mindset* became widely known through the work of psychologist **Dr. Carol Dweck**, who introduced the idea of *Fixed Mindset* versus *Growth Mindset*:

- **A Fixed Mindset** assumes our talents, intelligence, and emotional tendencies are unchangeable.
- **A Growth Mindset**, on the other hand, believes that we can develop ourselves with effort, learning, and time.

This distinction doesn't just affect how we approach learning, it has a direct impact on our happiness.

Scientific Insight: The Mindset-Happiness Link

Modern psychology and neuroscience have repeatedly shown that our beliefs about ourselves shape our emotions and behaviors. According to a study published in Nature, individuals who believed they had control over their emotions showed significantly higher well-being than those who felt their emotions were fixed. When you believe you can grow, bounce back, or choose your emotional focus, you begin to feel empowered. And empowerment is fertile ground for happiness to grow.

Coaching Reflection

"What's your dominant lens right now, criticism or compassion? Judgment or curiosity?"

Take a quiet moment and ask yourself:

- When things don't go as planned, do I blame myself… or look for a lesson?
- Do I believe others can grow, or do I secretly think people can't change?
- How do I talk to myself when I make a mistake?

These reflections matter. Because your mindset doesn't just shape how you see the world, it shapes the world you live in.

Example: The Two Colleagues

Consider this true story from one of my workshops: Two professionals, Rina and Aditya, received critical feedback from their manager during performance review week.

- Rina took the feedback as personal failure. She spiraled into doubt, avoided further conversations, and disengaged from her work.
- Aditya took the same feedback as a growth challenge. He booked a follow-up with his manager, asked for clarity, and created a 30-day action plan.

Same feedback. Same manager. Totally different outcomes. What changed? Not the job. Not the feedback. The mindset.

3.2 The Science of Thought and Emotion

Let's take a deeper look into the engine room of your happiness, your brain. Because as much as happiness feels emotional, it is also deeply neurological. At the heart of this connection is a powerful idea called **neuroplasticity**, the brain's ability to change and adapt based on your thoughts and experiences. Your brain isn't a fixed machine; it's more like a living sculpture, constantly being shaped by your beliefs, focus, and choices.

Neuroplasticity: Your Brain is Always Listening

Every time you think a thought, your brain fires neurons. And the more you repeat a thought, the stronger that neural connection becomes. This means that:

- If you often focus on what's missing, your brain becomes wired for dissatisfaction.
- If you train yourself to focus on what's working, your brain becomes wired for contentment.

This is why mindset matters. It's not just about being positive, it's about building neural pathways that make happiness your brain's default setting.

A 2005 study by Dr. Richard Davidson at the University of Wisconsin showed that people who regularly practiced positive emotional habits, such as gratitude or compassion, demonstrated increased activity in the left prefrontal cortex, the area of the brain associated with resilience and joy.

Your thoughts aren't just reflections. They're instructions to your brain.

Framing: The Story You Tell Becomes the Reality You Live

Another psychological concept that plays a huge role in happiness is cognitive framing.

Imagine two people stuck in traffic:

- One says, "This is ruining my day. I will never catch up."
- The other says, "This gives me a few quiet moments to breathe. Maybe I can listen to that podcast."

Same traffic. Very different emotional outcomes. That's the power of framing. The story you tell yourself about your experience shapes how your brain processes it, and how your body feels it. In fact, Dr. Barbara Fredrickson's *Broaden and Build Theory* shows that when we adopt positive mental framing, our brains expand in creativity, problem-solving, and even immune strength. Negative framing, by contrast, narrows our attention and triggers the stress response.

Coaching Reflection

"Is this a fact, or just one version of the story?"

The next time you find yourself spiraling into stress or worry, pause and ask:

- "Is there another way to look at this?"
- "What else could this mean?"
- "What would my wisest, calmest self say about this moment?"

Mindset is not about denying difficulty. It's about reclaiming your authorship of how you process it.

3.3 Types of Mindsets that Foster Happiness

Not all mindsets are created equal. Some uplift us, giving us strength, hope, and emotional space to grow. Others hold us back, trapping us in cycles of fear, scarcity, or self-criticism. In my years of coaching professionals, one pattern has stood out consistently, those who cultivate certain core mindsets tend to experience greater happiness, resilience, and inner peace, regardless of their circumstances.

Let's explore the most powerful ones.

Growth Mindset: Believing You Can Learn, Not Just Win

Coined by Dr. Carol Dweck, a growth mindset is the belief that your abilities, intelligence, and emotional strength can be developed with effort and experience.

People with a growth mindset:

- View failures as learning opportunities
- Accept challenges with curiosity instead of fear
- Are more persistent when faced with setbacks

Compare that to a fixed mindset, which leads people to believe they are "stuck" with whatever talents or flaws they were born with. Fixed mindsets fear mistakes, they see them as personal verdicts, not data for improvement.

Coaching Reflection: "If you knew success was about learning, not proving, what would you try today?"

Self-Compassion Mindset: Your Inner Ally, Not Your Inner Critic

Self-compassion is the mindset of treating yourself like you would treat a dear friend. Psychologist Dr. Kristin Neff's research shows that people who practice self-compassion are more emotionally resilient, less anxious, and more motivated to improve, without the toxic effects of harsh self-judgment. Self-compassionate people typically report feeling more emotionally well-off and having better life satisfaction, as they overcome obstacles with an understanding and loving-of-self perspective. It can be considered a means of achieving happiness by cultivating a pleasant and welcoming relationship with oneself, leading to deeper and longer-lasting joy.

When you make a mistake:

- The critic says: "You're a failure."
- The coach says: "You slipped. What can we learn and improve?"

Self-compassion is not about letting yourself off the hook. It's about giving yourself the right fuel to grow. Guilt can be motivating. Shame never is.

Coaching Prompt: "Would you say this out loud to someone you love?"

Abundance Mindset: There's Enough, and You Are Enough

One of the most transformative shifts a busy professional can make, especially in a world of constant competition and comparison, is the move from scarcity thinking to an abundance mindset.

What is an Abundance Mindset?

Coined and popularized by Stephen Covey in the 7 Habits of Highly Effective People, an abundance mindset is the belief that life is rich with opportunity, that joy multiplies when shared, and that success is not a limited resource.

In this mindset:

- There is enough time.
- There is enough success.
- There is enough love.
- And most importantly: you are enough.

Contrast that with the scarcity mindset, which whispers:

- "If they win, I lose."
- "There's only one shot, don't miss it."
- "I must prove my worth constantly."

This kind of thinking leads to anxiety, burnout, envy, and even ethical compromises in the workplace. You can be performing well, but still feel like you're falling behind, because someone else seems to be ahead.

What Does Abundance Look Like in Real Life?

Professionals with an abundance mindset:

- Celebrate others' wins because success is not finite.
- Collaborate generously, knowing shared efforts create greater impact.
- Live more peacefully, because they're not always in survival or performance mode.
- Feel secure in their self-worth, rather than constantly chasing validation.

They focus on what they can give, rather than what they might miss out on.

Research Behind Abundance Thinking

Psychologist Robert Emmons, one of the world's leading researchers on gratitude, found that people who regularly express gratitude experience:

- Stronger immune systems
- Longer, more restful sleep
- Fewer feelings of isolation and loneliness
- Higher levels of optimism and connection

These are all linked to an abundant emotional framework, seeing life as full rather than lacking. Even neuroscience backs this up. Gratitude and abundance activate the ventromedial prefrontal cortex, the area associated with reward and positive emotions.

Coaching Reflection: Are You Operating from Scarcity?

Take a pause and ask yourself:

- Do I celebrate others, or secretly feel behind when they succeed?
- Do I focus more on what I lack than what I already have?
- Do I believe I am enough… even when I'm not performing?

Coaching Prompt: "You are not behind. You're on your own path."

Comparison is the thief of both joy and momentum. Reclaim yours by stepping into abundance.

Quick Actionables to Build Abundance Thinking

Practice	How to Apply It	Frequency
Gratitude Journaling	Write down 3 things you're grateful for, especially things that someone else might envy.	Daily
Celebrate a Peer's Win	Publicly or privately applaud someone else's success. Let it inspire you, not shrink you.	Weekly
Abundance Affirmation	Repeat: "There is enough. I am enough." Say it in moments of self-doubt.	As needed
Give Without Expectation	Help a colleague, share a resource, mentor someone, without tracking favors.	Monthly

Coaching Reminder: "You are not behind. You're on your own path."

Optimism vs. Toxic Positivity: The Real vs. the Masked

In the professional world, where performance matters and appearances are often curated, it's easy to confuse positivity with emotional strength. But not all positivity is healthy. There's a big difference between realistic optimism and toxic positivity.

What's the Difference?

Optimism	Toxic Positivity
Acknowledges pain and hardship but believes things can improve	Ignores or invalidates negative emotions ("Just think positive!")
Engages with problems while maintaining hope	Suppresses feelings and avoids vulnerability
Builds resilience	Breeds guilt, shame, and emotional fatigue

Realistic optimism doesn't deny challenges, it honors them, but refuses to be defeated by them. It is rooted in hope, backed by effort, and infused with emotional honesty.

Dr. Martin Seligman, father of Positive Psychology, showed through decades of research that optimistic people:

- Are more resilient in the face of setbacks
- Recover faster from illness and injury
- Perform better under stress in professional and personal life

In contrast, toxic positivity is the pressure to always be happy or upbeat. It can show up as:

- "Don't be sad, everything happens for a reason."
- "Just look on the bright side."
- "It could be worse."

These statements might sound harmless, but they often shut down real emotional processing.

Why It Matters for Busy Professionals

In fast-paced, high-pressure environments, there's often no space for vulnerability. Leaders and professionals are expected to "stay positive" and "keep it together." But suppressing real emotions leads to:

- Burnout
- Emotional disconnection
- Shallow relationships
- Reduced authenticity as a leader

Authentic optimism builds psychological safety, both within and around you.

Coaching Perspective

"Optimism is not ignoring the storm. It's remembering you have the strength to walk through it."

Or as Seligman suggests, it's the ability to interpret negative events as temporary, specific, and changeable, not as permanent, pervasive failures.

Quick Actionables

Action	Description	Frequency
Name your feelings	Instead of saying “I’m fine,” try: “I’m stressed, but I know I have handled this before.”	Daily Check-In
Practice ‘And’ Thinking	Say: “This is hard and I believe I will get through it,” instead of pretending it’s easy.	As Needed
Emotional Labeling	Pause and name your emotional state. Studies show this reduces its intensity.	Daily
Journaling Prompts	“What’s true, even if it’s hard?” → “What strength am I using to handle this?”	Weekly

Coaching Perspective: “Optimism is not ignoring the storm. It’s remembering you have the strength to walk through it.”

The Empowered Mindset: Ownership of Choice and Responsibility

One of the most empowering mindsets is this: “I may not control everything, but I always control my response.”

Victim mindset says: “This happened to me.”

Empowered mindset asks: “How do I grow through this?”

It’s not about blame. It’s about agency. Empowered people take accountability for their emotions, choices, and growth. This mindset fuels action instead of paralysis.

Key Insight: You don’t need to perfect these mindsets all at once. Just begin with awareness. Then shift a little, each day, through small inner conversations that build new mental habits.

3.4 The Happiness Set Point – Can We Really Rewire It?

For decades, psychologists believed that each of us has a "set point" for happiness, a baseline level of contentment we tend to return to, no matter what happens. Win the lottery? You'll likely feel elated… but only for a while. Face a major setback? Sadness hits hard, but eventually, most people bounce back.

This idea came from research by Sonja Lyubomirsky, Ed Diener, and Martin Seligman, suggesting that approximately:

- 50% of our happiness is genetically determined (our set point),
- 10% comes from life circumstances (job, income, relationships),
- and 40% depends on our daily thoughts and actions, our intentional activities.

So, here's the empowering truth:

You may not control your happiness set point, but you have full control over your happiness mindset.

Scientific Backing: You Can Rewire for Happiness

Neuroscientists like Dr. Rick Hanson have shown that "neurons that fire together, wire together." This means the more we focus on joy, gratitude, resilience, and self-kindness, the more those mental states become traits. In other words, what starts as a mindset practice becomes a mindset pattern, physically rewired into your brain. Even people with high genetic vulnerability to anxiety or negativity have shown measurable increases in happiness after practicing interventions like:

- Gratitude journaling
- Loving-kindness meditation
- Acts of kindness
- Cognitive reframing

Coaching Reflection: Are You Living on Autopilot?

Ask yourself honestly:

- "Am I acting out of habit… or out of conscious choice?"
- "Have I accepted a baseline of stress or cynicism without questioning it?"
- "What is one small daily practice that could shift my emotional baseline?"

Even 5 minutes a day of intentional emotional focus, like savoring a moment, offering a compliment, or writing down one small win, can shift the trajectory of your week.

Rewiring in Practice: The 21-Day Mindset Habit Loop

Here's a simple habit loop used by my clients→ coaches:

- **Trigger:** Start the day with a cue (e.g., brushing teeth).
- **Routine:** Pair it with a happiness habit (e.g., 3 gratitudes or an empowering affirmation).
- **Reward:** End with a smile, breath, or moment of calm, seal the circuit.

Repeat daily. Track for 21 days. You'll not only feel better, you'll start thinking better.

3.5 The Power of Positive Thinking

Let's be clear: positive thinking is not about ignoring reality. It's not pretending that everything is fine when it's not. It's about developing a mental lens that looks for what's working, what's possible, and what's worth learning, even when things are hard. For busy professionals, the quality of your thoughts is often the silent partner behind your outcomes. If you walk into meetings expecting conflict, if you brace every Monday like a battle, if you expect things to go wrong, you might be unconsciously shaping your reality to match that mental forecast. That's the power of mindset.

One starting point for positive thinking is **self-talk.** The ceaseless flow of unsaid ideas that go through your mind is known as self-talk. These instinctive ideas might be constructive or destructive. A portion of your self-talk is based on reason and logic, while other self-talk could result from assumptions you make based on incomplete knowledge or anticipations brought on by preconceived notions of what might occur. If the majority of your thoughts are negative, you probably have a pessimistic mindset. If the majority of your thoughts are positive, you probably think positively and are an optimist.

What Science Says About Positive Thinking

Research in positive psychology shows that positive thinking broadens your field of vision, mentally and emotionally. Dr. Barbara Fredrickson's Broaden-and-Build Theory explains that positive emotions expand our awareness and encourage novel, varied, and exploratory thoughts and actions. Over time, this builds our psychological and social resources, like resilience, adaptability, and meaningful relationships.

One famous study at the University of North Carolina showed that people who practiced daily positivity rituals were better at managing stress, solving problems, and building connections.

Furthermore, researchers continue to explore the effects of positive thinking and optimism on health. The potential health benefits include:

- Increased life span
- Lower rates of depression
- Lower levels of distress and pain
- Greater resistance to illnesses
- Better psychological and physical well-being
- Better cardiovascular health and lower risk of death from cardiovascular disease and stroke
- Reduced risk of death from cancer, respiratory conditions, and infections
- Better coping skills during hardships and times of stress

It's believed that upbeat and cheerful individuals typically lead healthier lifestyles that include increased physical exercise, a better diet, and abstinence from smoking and excessive alcohol consumption.

The Reframing Technique: Shift Your Thought → Shift Your State

When you're caught in a spiral of worry, frustration, or negative self-talk, use this:

The 3Rs Reframe Method

Recognise	**Recognize** the negative or limiting thought.
Reflect	**Reflect:** "What else could be true here?"
Reframe	**Reframe:** Replace it with a helpful, believable alternative thought.

Example:

"This project is going to fail."

→ Recognize: Negative forecasting.

→ Reflect: What else is true? I have overcome similar challenges before.

→ Reframe: "This will be tough, but I'm equipped to handle it step-by-step."

This is not toxic positivity, it's practical optimism.

Application for Busy Professionals

- **In leadership:** A leader who maintains a calm and positive outlook during uncertain times creates psychological safety for their team.
- **In sales:** A rep who believes they might close a deal is likelier to follow up with courage and authenticity than one who's convinced it's lost.
- **In personal wellbeing:** Someone who tells themselves "This week has a few good things in it" will notice those things, and emotionally benefit from them.

Coaching Reflection

"What if the way you describe your challenges… is more stressful than the challenge itself?"

Language matters. Thoughts matter. They become instructions your brain uses to build your day.

Focusing on Positive Thinking (Additional Strategies):

It is possible to learn how to think positively instead of negatively. You are, after all, forming a new habit, so while the procedure is easy, it does require some time and practice. The strategies listed below can help you think and act in a more upbeat and hopeful manner:

- **Determine what needs to be changed:** Identify the aspects of your life that you typically think adversely about, such as your job, your daily commute, life changes, or a relationship. You can begin modestly by concentrating on a single area to address it more constructively. Instead of thinking negatively, try thinking positively to help you manage your stress.

- **Examine yourself:** Throughout the day, take a moment to reflect on your thoughts. If you discover that the majority of your thoughts are negative, attempt to find a method to frame them in a positive light.

- **Allow humor to enter your life:** Permit yourself to chuckle or grin, especially when things are tough. Find humor in ordinary events, even any small embarrassing moments in your life. Life feels less stressed when you can laugh at it.

- **Maintain a healthy lifestyle:** On most days of the week, try to get at least 30 minutes or more of exercise. Stress can be decreased and mood can be improved by exercise. Maintain a nutritious diet to power your body and mind. Make time to sleep. And pick up stress-reduction strategies.

- **Be in the company of positive people:** Ensure the individuals in your life are kind, encouraging people you can trust to offer insightful counsel and constructive criticism. Negative people can make you feel more stressed out and doubt your capacity to handle stress in healthy ways.

- **Engage in constructive self-talk:** Begin by adhering to one basic guideline: never say anything to yourself that you wouldn't say to someone else. Be kind and supportive of yourself. When a negative idea arises, consider it objectively and counter it with positive self-affirmations. Consider the blessings in your life for which you are grateful.

3.6 Mindfulness and Happiness

Mindfulness: A Process of Engagement with Happiness

Let's pause.

Take one full breath. Just notice it.

That moment, simple, still, and present, is mindfulness in action. And for busy professionals, learning to engage with life as it's happening, not just racing through it, can be a gateway to deeper happiness.

Mindfulness is defined as the consciousness that comes through paying attention to purpose, developing non-judgmental attention or self-regulation of attention towards one's experiences in the present moment with curiosity, aim, attitude, openness, and acceptance. Numerous studies indicate that optimal adaptation, which includes happiness or well-being, is positively correlated with mindfulness, and that mindfulness may even directly increase happiness. Therefore, it can be claimed that happiness is a tangible objective or result of human life and that it can only be attained through a sound acceptance of life's accomplishments and fulfillment.

From an evolutionary standpoint, human needs and emotions have developed to support the selection of adaptive behaviors that lead to happiness. A recent study by Geber and Wedberg explored the relationship between survival adaptation and happiness, suggesting psychologists should integrate positive psychology and evolutionary principles to help people live happier lives. Furthermore, through this integration of information, people's lives can also be improved by researching the elements that lead to happier and more fulfilling lives.

What Is Mindfulness?

Mindfulness is the practice of bringing your full attention to the present moment, with openness and without judgment. It's not about emptying your mind or becoming a monk. It's about showing up fully in your life, even in the ordinary moments. Whether you're sipping coffee, attending a meeting, walking to your car, or reading this page, you can train your attention to be here. When you do, stress levels drop, clarity improves, emotional reactivity decreases, and, importantly, happiness becomes more accessible.

The Science Behind Mindfulness and Happiness

Studies from Harvard, Yale, and Oxford have repeatedly shown that people who are more mindful are significantly happier, regardless of age, gender, or job.

One landmark Harvard study found that "a wandering mind is an unhappy mind." They discovered that almost 47% of the time, people are not paying attention to what they're doing, and this lack of presence correlated with lower happiness scores.

Another study published in Psychosomatic Medicine showed that just 8 weeks of mindfulness training significantly reduced stress and boosted positive affect, even in high-stress jobs.

Why it Works for Busy Professionals

- It gives you mental space between stimulus and response, especially in high-stakes decisions.
- It strengthens your focus, cutting through distractions so you can work deeper in less time.
- It creates moments of restoration, without needing long breaks or time off.

Mindfulness isn't a break from productivity. It's a better way to be productive, with your mind, body, and heart aligned.

Practical Mindfulness Exercises for Your Day

- **The Mindful Minute:** Pause. Close your eyes. Inhale for 4, hold for 4, exhale for 4. Do this for 1 minute. Notice the shift.
- **Mindful Walking:** On your way to the next meeting or call, pay attention to your steps. Notice the rhythm. Feel your feet on the ground.

- The STOP Method:

S – Stop what you're doing

T – Take a breath

O – Observe what's happening (thoughts, body, surroundings)

P – Proceed with clarity

- **Mindful Listening in Conversations:** Don't plan your response while someone is talking. Just listen, fully. People feel it. And it transforms how you're received.

Coaching Prompt

"Are you living your day… or just managing it?"

Mindfulness reconnects you with your life in real time. And that's where joy often hides, not in big achievements, but in small moments we were present enough to feel.

3.7 Gratitude and Happiness

The Hidden Power of Thankfulness in Daily Life

Imagine waking up tomorrow and only having the things you were grateful for today. It's a humbling, powerful thought, and one that reflects the deep psychological and emotional power of gratitude. Gratitude isn't just a pleasant sentiment; it's a practice, a lens, and a muscle that when strengthened, can dramatically shift how you experience your life, even as a busy professional.

What is Gratitude?

At its core, gratitude is the conscious acknowledgment of goodness, noticing, appreciating, and internalizing the positive. It may be directed toward people, experiences, situations, or even the simple fact that you're alive and breathing. It says: "There is something good here, even now."

Robert Emmons, one of the foremost authorities on gratitude, explains: "It's an affirmation of goodness. We affirm that there are good things in the world, gifts and benefits we have received." It is a positive emotional response that fulfills a biological need. Importantly, gratitude is not blind positivity. It doesn't deny problems. Instead, it creates a balanced emotional baseline from which you can respond more wisely to both challenges and successes.

What Science Says About Gratitude

Gratitude has been extensively studied by psychologists like Dr. Robert Emmons and Dr. Martin Seligman. Their research shows that:

- People who practice gratitude daily experience 25% greater happiness than those who don't.
- Gratitude improves sleep quality, reduces stress hormones, and enhances immune function.
- A single gratitude letter, even if not sent, has been shown to elevate mood for weeks.
- Those who journal things they are grateful for report higher levels of energy, optimism, and connection to others.

In short: Gratitude rewires the brain. When practiced regularly, it actually increases gray matter in areas of the brain associated with emotional regulation and reward.

Gratitude is a Key to Happiness: 4 Reasons Why

Happiness can occasionally seem elusive, particularly during difficult circumstances. However, gratitude or thankfulness offers a surprisingly simple route to happiness, contentment, and optimism. Ironically, the pursuit of happiness itself can sometimes backfire, drawing attention to what you lack. Conversely, cultivating thankfulness usually leads to higher levels of happiness. Here's why:

- **Relationships:** Research conducted at the University of Montana revealed that individuals who showed greater thankfulness also tended to report higher levels of happiness, heavily influenced by how connections between people were impacted by appreciation. When people show their gratitude and hear others express gratitude, they often feel better about themselves and other people. Research from the University of New South Wales found respondents were more inclined to believe they might have a meaningful relationship with someone after hearing them express thanks.

- **Experiences and Materialism:** Gratitude also influences how we spend our time and money. Researchers at Cornell University discovered that consumers were more likely to exhibit enjoyment when they wrote good evaluations about great experiences than when they wrote reviews about purchases. Experiencing something new necessitates deeper processing that allows one to go back on and relive the moment, solidifying enjoyment. We also generally enjoy our encounters with other people; spending time with them, making an investment in their connection, and the dynamics of sharing all contribute to happiness.
- **Giving Back and Giving Voice:** The Cornell University study also discovered that individuals were more likely to be motivated to act altruistically in the future and enhance the pleasure of others when they thought back on their positive experiences. In addition to inspiring happiness, gratitude also motivates people to want to make their community a happier place. Giving voice to one's thankfulness and expressing it also appears to indicate happier lives; a Kent State Study found participants were more likely to report feeling happy when they were able to express their gratitude.
- **A Genetic Component:** Perhaps the most intriguing finding is that happiness and thankfulness or gratitude have a genetic component. According to author, Jonathan Haidt, circumstances, decisions, and a genetic predisposition, all have a role in happiness. New research from the University of Arkansas suggests a "gratitude gene," with those possessing it reporting greater appreciation for their spouse, happier marriages, greater forgiveness, and greater faith. While this evidence comes from marriage, this gene relates to other partnerships as well. Your decisions also play a significant role in developing these traits.

Why Gratitude is a Game-Changer for Busy Professionals

Most professionals live in a goal-driven world, one that often emphasizes what's next, what's missing, and what needs fixing. Gratitude interrupts this loop. It shifts your focus from the deficit mindset to the abundance mindset.

When you practice gratitude:

- Meetings become opportunities, not obligations.
- Teammates become sources of support, not stress.
- Deadlines become proof of trust, not pressure.

Gratitude restores meaning to moments that would otherwise pass unnoticed.

Simple Gratitude Practices That Fit Busy Lives

Here are actionable ways to integrate gratitude into your daily rhythm, no meditation cushion required:

1. **The 3-Blessings Journal (2 mins at night):** Every night, write down three good things that happened today, and why they happened. This deepens the emotional impact and helps your brain start scanning for more.
2. **Gratitude Trigger Anchors:** Choose a daily habit (like brushing teeth, morning coffee, or logging into email) and pair it with mentally naming one thing you're grateful for. This builds an unconscious habit loop.
3. **One-Minute Gratitude Text:** Send a quick message to a colleague, friend, or family member, expressing appreciation for something specific they've done. It will boost both your mood and theirs.
4. **Gratitude Wall (Team Edition):** In your team, create a shared gratitude board (physical or digital). Start meetings by acknowledging someone's contribution. It lifts morale and strengthens relationships.
5. **Gratitude Reframe:** When facing a challenge, ask: "What is this teaching me that I will be grateful for later?" This creates a cognitive reframe in real-time.

Coaching Reflection

"When was the last time you paused to feel grateful for something you now take for granted?"

Gratitude softens your inner world. It's not a luxury, it's an emotional necessity in high-paced lives. It brings perspective, humility, and connection back into focus.

3.8 Self-Compassion and Happiness

Why Being Kinder to Yourself is the Missing Key to Long-Term Fulfillment

Many high-achieving professionals speak to themselves in ways they'd never speak to a friend:

"You're so stupid."

"You always mess things up."

"You're not doing enough."

This inner critic, often mistaken as a motivator, is actually a happiness thief. What's needed instead is self-compassion, not as weakness or indulgence, but as a core psychological skill that enables resilience, clarity, and sustainable happiness.

What is Self-Compassion?

Self-compassion is the practice of treating yourself with the same understanding and support you'd offer a close friend going through a hard time. According to Dr. Kristin Neff, the pioneer of this concept, self-compassion has three main components:

- **Self-Kindness:** Being warm and understanding toward ourselves when we fail, rather than harshly self-critical.

- **Common Humanity:** Recognizing that suffering and personal inadequacy is part of the shared human experience, not something that isolates us.
- **Mindfulness:** Holding our thoughts and emotions in balanced awareness, rather than over-identifying with them.

In essence, self-compassion is not letting yourself off the hook, it's keeping yourself in the loop of love and understanding. People who practice self-compassion are more capable of overcoming obstacles in life. Rather than moping around apparent shortcomings, they tackle challenges with an understanding and loving-of-self perspective. This kind of mindset establishes the groundwork for happiness in addition to better mental health.

The Science of Self-Compassion and Wellbeing

Dozens of studies show that people who practice self-compassion experience:

- Lower levels of stress and anxiety
- Better emotional resilience
- Stronger relationships
- Greater life satisfaction and self-worth

A 2012 study from the University of Arizona found that self-compassion predicts happiness more strongly than self-esteem. And while self-esteem can fluctuate with achievement or comparison, self-compassion is steady. It's available even when you fail.

Positive psychology research backs up the idea that self-compassion and happiness are related. Research indicates that those who engage in self-compassion practices not only have greater resilience in the face of misfortune but also demonstrate elevated levels of life pleasure. Being able to be nice and understanding to oneself starts a positive feedback loop that makes life seem more promising.

Why It Matters for Busy Professionals

Many professionals operate with high expectations and minimal rest. They feel they must earn happiness, and if they fall short, they punish themselves internally.

But here's the paradox: The harder you are on yourself… the less likely you are to grow, lead well, or enjoy your life.

Self-compassion gives you mental space to learn from mistakes without being emotionally crushed by them. It helps you bounce back, not break down.

Tools to Practice Self-Compassion

1. The Self-Compassion Break (90 seconds):

Pause when you're upset. Silently say to yourself:

- "This is a moment of struggle." (Mindfulness)
- "Struggle is part of being human." (Common humanity)
- "May I be kind to myself in this moment." (Self-kindness)

This simple ritual disrupts the inner critic and replaces it with emotional grounding.

2. Rewrite the Inner Script:

Write down a recent moment when you were self-critical. Then, rewrite what you wish someone kind had told you. Read that aloud. Over time, this rewires your inner dialogue.

3. Practice 'Name It to Tame It':

When you feel overwhelmed, instead of judging yourself, try naming the emotion:

"I feel anxious."

"I'm disappointed."

This reduces its grip on you and builds mindful self-regulation.

4. Ask: "What Would I Say to a Friend?":

Literally pause and ask yourself:

"If my best friend were going through this, what would I tell them?" Then say that to yourself.

Coaching Reflection

"Are you motivated by love… or by fear of falling short?"

Self-compassion is the foundation that allows joy to grow, not as a reward, but as a rightful part of your journey.

3.9 Practical Tools to Reset and Strengthen Mindset

Mindset isn't just a trait, it's a trainable muscle. Much like physical fitness, mental fitness comes not from one-time inspiration, but from small, repeatable practices. As a coach, I have seen how even the busiest professionals can shift their mindset, and their happiness, by making room for a few powerful habits.

Daily Rituals for Mental Clarity, Emotional Resilience, and Sustainable Joy

Think of your mindset like a muscle. You can't build it once and be done. It needs regular exercise, especially in the demanding life of a busy professional. This section offers a practical, no-fluff toolkit. These tools don't require hours of free time, just intention, consistency, and self-kindness.

Tool 1: Thought Reframing – The Art of the Second Look

We all have automatic thoughts, the first thought, that surface quickly, often driven by fear or past conditioning. But your true power lies in the second thought, the conscious choice to view the situation with perspective and self-leadership.

Example:

First Thought: "I totally messed up the meeting."

Second Thought: "That was a tough moment, but I did my best under pressure. I'm learning and growing."

How to Practice:

- **Notice:** When you feel upset or discouraged, pause and identify the thought.
- **Challenge:** Ask, "Is this 100% true?" or "Would I say this to a friend?"
- **Reframe:** Choose a more empowering version of that thought.

Coaching Prompt: "Are you feeding your inner critic, or your inner coach?"

Tool 2: Daily Journaling – The 3Q Reflection

Journaling isn't about writing essays. It's about creating space for awareness.

Every evening, answer these 3Qs:

- What went well today? (Reinforces positivity)
- What challenged me today? (Builds awareness)
- What will I carry forward tomorrow? (Creates intention)

Why it works: This short ritual rewires your mind to scan for progress instead of perfection. Even 5 minutes can build mental clarity and emotional balance.

Tool 3: Morning Mindset Priming Ritual

Before jumping into notifications, shape your mental tone intentionally.

3-minute ritual:

- Close your eyes. Take 3 slow, deep breaths.
- Ask: "How do I want to feel today?"
- Visualize one small win that would help you feel that way. (e.g., calm = a peaceful commute, confident = making your point in a meeting)

Why it works: This simple act of priming shifts your mindset from reactive to purposeful.

Tool 4: Midday Mindset Reset Break

Stress accumulates during the day. If you don't reset, your default mode takes over.

Try this at 2 PM (set a reminder):

- Pause. Put one hand on your chest.
- Breathe deeply. Ask:
    - "What story am I telling myself right now?"
    - "What else might be true?"
- Choose a more helpful story and return to your task.

Why it works: It clears emotional fog and lets you lead from your center, not your chaos.

Tool 5: Weekly Self Check-In

Once a week, scan your energy and alignment, not your calendar.

On Sunday evening or Monday morning, ask:

- What fueled my energy last week?
- What drained it?
- Where did I act from self-doubt?
- Where did I lead with confidence and trust?

Reminder: "You don't need more time. You need more alignment."

Tool 6: The 5-Day Reframing Challenge

Build mindset muscle in just 5 days:

Day	Practice
1	Write 3 self-critical thoughts. Reframe each with kindness.
2	Take one challenge. Write 3 alternate interpretations.
3	Rewrite a past failure as a growth story.
4	Turn a complaint into gratitude. ("I get to...")
5	Visualize your 6-month future self. How would they think?

Why it works: This structured challenge boosts mental agility and turns hardship into insight.

Tool 7: The 3-Minute Morning Reset

Especially useful for days with early meetings or mental fog.

Steps:

- Sit upright with feet on the floor.
- Inhale for 4, hold for 4, exhale for 6 (repeat 3 times).
- Say: "What do I want to embody today?" Write it down.

Why it works: Prevents your mind from spiraling into urgency and anchors you in calm.

Tool 8: Catch-and-Reframe Habit

Create a mental intercept system throughout the day.

How:

- Any time you notice tension, stop.
- Name the emotion. ("I feel frustrated.")
- Ask: "What is another way I could view this moment?"
- Practice saying that new sentence out loud.

Why it works: Thoughts shape feelings. Reframing prevents your brain from looping into stress.

Tool 9: Mindset Meal Check-In

Pair nourishment with mental tuning.

During lunch or dinner, ask:

- One thing I'm doing well today
- One limiting belief I can release today

Why it works: Associating positive mindset shifts with everyday habits builds consistency.

Tool 10: 5-Minute Mindful Reset

Need to bounce back after a tough conversation or a Zoom marathon?

Steps:

- Find a quiet space or put on headphones.
- Inhale 4, hold 4, exhale 6 (repeat).
- Count 10 breaths and start over if distracted.

Why it works: A short mindfulness burst activates your parasympathetic nervous system, calming your mind and body.

Tool 11: Self-Compassion Mirror Exercise

Turn the mirror into a tool of support.

Daily or as needed:

Look into your eyes and say:

"I'm learning. I'm enough. I deserve patience."

Why it works: Over time, this practice retrains your self-dialogue to be supportive, not punitive.

Tool 12: Gratitude Microburst

A 30-second joy booster.

How:

- Set an alarm for 3:33 PM.
- When it goes off, pause and name:
    - One thing you're grateful for
    - One person you appreciate
    - One thing you're proud of

Why it works: Quick gratitude bursts elevate emotional set-points and reduce stress.

Tool 13: 5-Sense Grounding Technique

Use your body to regulate your thoughts.

Steps (say each aloud or in your mind):

- 5 things I see
- 4 things I feel
- 3 things I hear
- 2 things I smell
- 1 thing I taste

Why it works: Engages the sensory brain and brings you out of panic into the present.

Tool 14: Values Reminder Card

Recenter your decisions and mindset on what truly matters.

Create a pocket card or phone note with 3 core values (e.g., Kindness, Growth, Simplicity).

Before tough conversations or big choices, glance at it.

Why it works: Anchors your behavior in authenticity and direction, not external approval or pressure.

Final Thought: "You don't need to master all 14. Just choose one or two to begin, and make them a daily act of self-respect."

3.10 Key Learnings + Quick Actionables

Let's bring it all together. This chapter explored how mindset is not just a filter through which we see the world, it's the very architecture of our happiness. The way we think becomes the way we feel. The way we feel becomes the way we live.

Below are the Key Learnings and Quick Actionables for busy professionals who wish to strengthen their mindset for sustained happiness, even amidst pressure, deadlines, and complexity.

Key Learnings

- **Mindset is Trainable:** You're not stuck with the way you think. Neuroplasticity proves we can rewire emotional patterns with practice.
- **Your Mindset Filters Reality:** Your thoughts shape not just your interpretation of events, but your emotional and physiological response to them.
- **Growth-Oriented Mindsets Lead to Greater Joy:** Practices like optimism, self-compassion, and abundance fuel more sustainable well-being than reactive, fear-based thinking.
- **You Can Influence Your Happiness Baseline:** While some aspects of happiness are genetic, your mindset and habits play a larger role than most realize.
- **Mindset Is a Daily Choice:** Just like brushing your teeth or checking email, happiness is built through small, intentional mental routines.

Quick actionable for Busy Professionals

Frequency	Actionable Practice	Category
Daily	Begin your day with a 3-minute Mindset Priming ritual	Emotional Framing
Daily	Reframe one negative thought using a supportive voice	Self-Compassion
Daily	Pause mid-day and ask: "What else could be true?"	Stress Recovery
Daily	Write one thing you're proud of today	Growth Mindset
Weekly	Do a 3Q Journal Reflection (What went well? What challenged me? What will I carry forward?)	Self-Awareness
Weekly	Take a "Mindset Walk" (walk + one new empowering thought)	Somatic Reset
Weekly	Perform a 5-minute visualization of a future version of yourself	Motivation Boost
Monthly	Complete the 5-Day Reframing Challenge	Habit Reinforcement
Monthly	Revisit and rate your dominant mindset types	Meta-Reflection
Monthly	Discuss mindset shifts with a coach, friend, or peer	Accountability

3.11 Additional Resources for Cultivating a Happiness Mindset

As a busy professional, you may not have hours to sift through dense material, but a few targeted, powerful resources can transform your mindset. Below is a carefully curated list of books, talks, podcasts, and digital tools, each one selected for its clarity, accessibility, and deep alignment with the themes of this chapter. You'll find science-backed insights, practical strategies, and deeply engaging perspectives that reinforce everything we have explored.

Books You Can Explore

- **Mindset: The New Psychology of Success** – by Dr. Carol S. Dweck

  Learn how the growth mindset can change your approach to learning, failure, and leadership.

- **The Happiness Advantage** – by Shawn Achor

  A lively, research-based look at how happiness fuels success (not the other way around).

- **Self-Compassion: The Proven Power of Being Kind to Yourself** – by Dr. Kristin Neff

  A brilliant and gentle guide to silencing the inner critic and fostering emotional strength.

- **Hardwiring Happiness** – by Dr. Rick Hanson

  Discover how to reprogram your brain for calm, confidence, and contentment using simple daily practices.

TED Talks & Audio Learning

1. **"The Happy Secret to Better Work" – Shawn Achor (TED Talk)** https://www.ted.com/talks/shawn_achor_the_happy_secret_to_better_work
2. **"The Power of Believing That You Can Improve" – Dr. Carol Dweck (TED Talk)** https://www.ted.com/talks/carol_dweck_the_power_of_believing_that_you_can_improve
3. **The Happiness Lab Podcast – by Dr. Laurie Santos** Podcast episodes grounded in science and made for busy, curious minds.
   https://www.happinesslab.fm/

Digital Tools & Apps (Android & iOS)

1. **Mood Meter by Yale Center for Emotional Intelligence** Helps track your emotions and build emotional literacy. https://moodmeterapp.com/

2. **Gratitude – Journal & Reminders App**
   Build the habit of daily gratitude in just 5 minutes.
   https://gratefulness.me/gratitude-app/

3. **Insight Timer (Free Meditation & Mindfulness App)**
   Offers short guided practices to reset your mindset throughout the day.
   https://insighttimer.com/

4. **Calm App** (Premium, with some free features)
   Excellent for short breaks, visualizations, and focus building.
   https://www.calm.com/

References & Resources

- Counting Blessings Versus Burdens: An Experimental Investigation of Gratitude and Subjective Well-Being in Daily Life
- The 7 Habits of Highly Effective People
- The Effects of Gratitude Expression on Neural Activity
- Seligman, M.E.P. (2006). Learned Optimism: How to Change Your Mind and Your Life.
- Learned Optimism: How to Change Your Mind and Your Life
- The Cultural Costs of Happiness: The Impact of Mandating Happiness in the Workplace
- Resilient Individuals Use Positive Emotions to Bounce Back from Negative Emotional Experiences

Part 2:
Building Happiness

Chapter 4:

Daily Habits that Shape our Joy & Happiness

4.1 Daily Habits That Shape Our Joy

"We are what we repeatedly do.
Happiness, then, is not an act, but a habit."

4.2 The Power of Daily Habits for Busy Professionals

In the modern professional's world, time is scarce, deadlines are plenty, and the line between work and life often blurs. Amidst this whirlwind, happiness can feel like a distant luxury, something we will focus on "once things settle down." But here's the truth: your daily habits are already shaping your happiness, whether intentionally or not.

Just as stress, poor sleep, or skipping meals can nudge us toward burnout, small, repeated acts of wellness can nudge us back to joy. This chapter is not about major life overhauls or unrealistic resolutions. It's about practical, research-backed habits that anyone, even the busiest professional, can adopt to build sustainable happiness, one day at a time.

Let's explore four of the most powerful levers:

- Movement
- Nutrition
- Rest
- Joyful engagement

These are not just physical practices. They are emotional investments, into your energy, mood, relationships, and self-worth.

4.3 Exercise and Physical Activity – A Direct Line to Joy

"You're only one workout away from a better mood."

This is not just motivational poster fluff, it's neuroscience.

The Brain on Movement

When we move our bodies, our brains light up. Endorphins flood our system, offering a natural high. Dopamine boosts motivation. Serotonin improves mood and reduces anxiety. BDNF (Brain-Derived Neurotrophic Factor) helps neurons grow and strengthens memory and learning. This powerful mix rewires our brain toward resilience and positivity.

In fact, a study published in Psychosomatic Medicine found that regular physical activity was as effective as antidepressants in reducing symptoms of mild to moderate depression. But you don't need a clinical diagnosis to benefit. Even a 20-minute brisk walk can elevate mood, sharpen focus, and restore perspective.

Movement That Fits Your Life

You don't need a gym membership or a personal trainer to feel the joy of movement. The key is consistency over intensity, and choosing forms of activity that bring delight, not dread.

Try these:

- Morning stretches or sun salutation for 5 minutes
- Walking phone calls during meetings
- Evening dance break with your child or partner
- 10-minute home yoga or HIIT session from YouTube
- Staircase gratitude walk: each step, name one thing you're thankful for

Busy Professional Reframe: "If you don't have time for 30 minutes of exercise, do 3 minutes ten times."

Coaching Reflection: "What kind of movement makes me feel most alive, not just fit?"

Quick Actionables:

Habit	Time Needed	Frequency
5-minute stretch in the morning	5 min	Daily
Walking meetings or calls	Varies	2–3x/week
1 joyful physical activity (e.g. dance, hike, sport)	30–60 min	Weekly

4.4 Healthy Eating – Fueling Your Mood, Not Just Your Body

"Every bite is either feeding your energy, or draining your joy."

Food isn't just fuel for your body, it's information for your brain, a regulator of mood, and a powerful ally in your happiness journey.

The Gut-Brain Connection

You've likely heard the phrase "gut feeling." Science backs it up. Your gut houses 100 million neurons and produces over 90% of your serotonin, the neurotransmitter responsible for happiness and emotional stability. This means what you eat literally impacts how you feel, think, and relate to others.

A study in Nutritional Neuroscience revealed that individuals who ate a Mediterranean-style diet, rich in vegetables, whole grains, nuts, and healthy fats, experienced lower rates of depression and anxiety than those on a standard processed diet.

The Happiness Plate

You don't need complicated meal plans or rigid rules. What you need is awareness and intention.

Here's what a "happiness-supporting" plate looks like:

- **Colors:** Aim for a variety of vegetables and fruits (each color = different mood-boosting micronutrients)
- **Fats:** Include brain-healthy fats like olive oil, nuts, seeds, and avocado
- **Proteins:** Support energy and neurotransmitter function with lentils, tofu, paneer, eggs, or lean meats
- **Complex Carbs:** Whole grains and legumes help stabilize mood and blood sugar
- **Water:** Even slight dehydration can cause irritability and fatigue

But What About Comfort Food?

You don't need to eliminate indulgences. In fact, deprivation can decrease happiness. Instead:

- Eat mindfully: Enjoy treats slowly, without guilt
- Balance the plate: Add something nutritious alongside the indulgence
- Tune in: How does that food make you feel 30 minutes later?

Coaching Reflection:

"Which foods make me feel vibrant, energized, and emotionally steady?"

"Which ones spike my mood temporarily but leave me drained?"

Quick Actionables:

Habit	Time Needed	Frequency
Add 1 extra vegetable to any main meal	2 min	Daily
Hydration check-in (aim for 8 glasses)	5 sec reminders	Daily
Try 1 new whole food recipe	30–40 min	Weekly
Mindful eating pause (3 deep breaths before eating)	30 sec	Daily

4.5 Sleep – The Forgotten Pillar of Happiness

"Sleep is the golden chain that ties health and happiness together." – Thomas Dekker

We often treat sleep like a luxury. In truth, it's non-negotiable fuel for emotional strength, focus, and joy. In a high-performance life, sleep is not the cost of ambition, it is the foundation of sustainable success.

The Science: How Sleep Protects Your Mood

During sleep, your brain:

- Processes emotional experiences
- Flushes out stress hormones
- Recharges memory, focus, and decision-making capacity

- Rebalances neurotransmitters like dopamine and serotonin

Studies published in journals like Sleep Health and The Lancet Psychiatry show that chronic sleep deprivation increases the risk of anxiety, depression, and emotional reactivity. Even one night of poor sleep can impair emotional regulation by 60%, according to research from UC Berkeley.

Stages of Sleep That Matter

- **NREM Deep Sleep:** Physical restoration, tissue repair, immune strengthening

- **REM Sleep:** Dreaming, emotional processing, memory integration

Both stages are vital. Skipping them leads to emotional fatigue and lower happiness, even if you're "functioning."

Napping: The Midday Mindset Reset

Naps aren't laziness, they're brain optimization. A 20-minute power nap can restore alertness and elevate mood without grogginess. It's the emotional equivalent of turning your laptop off and on again.

Coaching Reflection:

"Am I sleeping to survive, or sleeping to thrive?"

"How differently do I show up when I have slept well?"

Quick Actionables:

Habit	Time Needed	Frequency
Set a fixed bedtime (+/- 30 mins)	2 min planning	Daily
Digital detox 45 mins before bed	45 min	Daily
Try a 20-min nap (post-lunch)	20 min	As needed (2–3x/week)
Create a wind-down ritual (stretch, tea, gratitude)	10–15 min	Daily

4.6 Hobbies and Leisure – The Joy of Doing Just Because

"Happiness lies in the joy of achievement, and the thrill of creative effort." – Franklin D. Roosevelt

In a world obsessed with productivity, hobbies can feel indulgent. But the science, and lived experience, says otherwise. Leisure isn't a luxury. It's a psychological necessity.

Why Leisure Matters for Your Emotional Well-being

Engaging in leisure activities, whether it's painting, gardening, music, or even solving puzzles, activates what psychologists call "flow states." Flow is a mental zone of deep focus, creativity, and pleasure where time disappears and joy expands.

According to a study in the Annals of Behavioural Medicine, people who engaged in hobbies experienced lower cortisol (stress hormone) levels, improved mood, and a greater sense of meaning in life, even when done just once a week.

Play for the Sake of Play

Not everything has to serve your resume. Some things should serve your soul. Rediscover the joy of:

- Sketching or crafting without goals
- Playing an instrument with no audience
- Learning something new, just for curiosity
- Weekly game nights or nature walks

These are not distractions. They are reconnections, to your essence, your energy, and your childlike joy.

Coaching Reflection:

"What activity makes me lose track of time?"

"What did I once love that I stopped doing because life got 'too busy'?"

Quick Actionables:

Habit	Time Needed	Frequency
Revisit 1 childhood hobby	30–60 min	Weekly
Schedule "No-Guilt Leisure Time" in your calendar	15–30 min	2–3x/week
Try a new skill/hobby via YouTube/online	30–45 min	Monthly
Create a "Joy Jar" of small leisure ideas to pull from	10 min setup	Ongoing

4.7 The Art of Doing Nothing – Reclaiming Rest as a Radical Act

> *"Sometimes the most productive thing you can do is rest."*
>
> – Mark Black

In a culture that glorifies busyness, simply doing nothing can feel rebellious. But true happiness often hides in the quiet spaces between achievements. It's in the unstructured moments, a quiet afternoon sunbeam, a slow sip of chai, a gaze at the sky, that our nervous systems reset and our soul exhales.

Doing nothing is not laziness. It's a form of active presence, letting your mind unfurl, your emotions settle, and your creativity bubble back up. Studies show that periods of intentional rest improve emotional regulation, memory consolidation, and even problem-solving.

Try this: Sit with no phone, no agenda, no distraction, for 10 minutes. Just breathe. Watch your thoughts come and go like clouds. No fixing. No forcing. Just being.

You don't always have to be "on" to be enough.

Coaching Reflection:

"When was the last time I allowed myself to simply be?"

"What might I gain if I stopped doing for just a little while?"

4.8 Key Learnings + Quick Actionables

Key Learnings

- **Happiness is habit-driven:** Lasting joy doesn't arise from major events, it is cultivated through small, consistent, daily choices that align with your energy and values.
- **Physical activity is emotional medicine:** Movement fuels not just the body, but also the mind, boosting endorphins, reducing stress, and enhancing mental clarity.
- **What you eat affects how you feel:** Food influences your mood, focus, and resilience through powerful gut-brain pathways.
- **Sleep is the foundation, not the reward:** Quality rest is directly tied to emotional strength, decision-making, and long-term joy.
- **Leisure is not a luxury, it's a lifeline:** Hobbies and moments of unstructured joy reconnect us with play, purpose, and presence.
- **Stillness heals:** The art of doing nothing helps busy professionals slow down, reset the mind, and reconnect with inner calm.

Quick Actionables for Busy Professionals

Action	Time Needed	Frequency
Morning 5-min stretch	5 min	Daily
Midday mindset reset (deep breath, thought check-in)	2 min	Daily
Add 1 new veggie to lunch or dinner	2 min	Daily
Mindful eating pause (3 breaths before meals)	30 sec	Daily
Set fixed bedtime + wind-down ritual	10–15 min	Daily
Try 1 joyful physical activity (walk, dance, sport)	30–60 min	Weekly
Revisit 1 hobby or explore a new one	30–60 min	Weekly
Schedule "No-Guilt Leisure" in calendar	15–30 min	2–3x/week
Try a 20-min nap (when energy dips)	20 min	1–2x/week
Sit in silence with no agenda	10 min	Weekly
Weekly reflection journal (What fueled/drained me?)	10 min	Weekly
"Joy Jar" – Create a list of low-effort happy habits	15 min setup	Ongoing

Chapter 5:

Emotions & Happiness – A Revised Draft

5.1 Emotional Mastery and Inner Peace

> *"Between stimulus and response, there is a space. In that space is our power to choose our response. In our response lies our growth and our freedom."*
>
> — Viktor E. Frankl

In today's demanding professional world, emotional mastery is not a luxury—it's leadership. It's clarity in chaos. It's the difference between reacting and responding, between spiraling and staying centered. True happiness often comes from navigating life's inherent obstacles with grace and **building resilience, the capacity to recover from setbacks.**

Most professionals are taught to master strategy, time, and technology. But those who rise above the rest—those who lead with grace, adapt with confidence, and inspire others—have mastered something more fundamental: their inner emotional landscape.

5.2 Understanding Emotions vs. Moods

Before we can master anything, we must first understand it.

- **Emotions** are short-term, intense responses to a specific trigger. They rise, peak, and fade.

Example: You feel anger when a colleague interrupts you.

- **Moods** are longer-lasting emotional states, often without a clear trigger.
    - *Example:* You feel low for a few hours without knowing why.

Understanding this distinction empowers us to:

- Label what we're experiencing accurately
- Stop "mood drift" from affecting our behavior
- Intervene before emotional hijack

Coaching Insight: "Am I reacting to this moment—or to a mood that started hours ago?"

5.3 Why Emotional Regulation is the New Superpower

Modern neuroscience shows that emotional self-regulation is one of the top predictors of:

- Effective leadership
- Resilient mental health
- Deep, fulfilling relationships

Cultivating habits like mindfulness and fostering strong social ties are foundational to this resilience, enabling people to face hardships without being overly impacted by them. Studies from Yale's Center for Emotional Intelligence and Harvard Business Review show that professionals with high emotional regulation:

- Make better decisions under stress
- Have stronger team rapport
- Experience significantly lower burnout

But here's the truth: we were never taught how to regulate emotions. We were told to suppress, distract, or "move on." It's time to change that narrative.

5.4 Practical Tools for Emotional Mastery

Especially curated for busy professionals navigating pressure, decisions, and people dynamics daily.

Tool 1: Emotional Labeling – "Name it to Tame it"

When emotions are unspoken, they tend to hijack us. But when you name the feeling, you engage your prefrontal cortex (thinking brain), which calms the amygdala (emotional brain).

Neuroscience Insight: Research by Dr. Matthew Lieberman (UCLA) showed that simply labeling emotions—"I feel frustrated" instead of "I'm fine"—reduces activity in the emotional centers of the brain and improves emotional control.

How to Apply (30 Seconds):

- Pause. Ask: "What exactly am I feeling right now?"
- Use specific words: Overwhelmed? Ashamed? Anxious? Curious?
- Say it aloud or write it down.

Coaching Reflection: "What's the most honest word for what I'm feeling?"

Practice Self-Compassion: When facing challenges or setbacks, being nice and empathetic to yourself lowers self-criticism and increases emotional resilience. Treat yourself with the same care and understanding you would show a trusted friend, rather than passing judgment or offering criticism. Accepting that mistakes are a part of the human experience makes it easier to face obstacles head-on.

Tool 2: Thought + Feeling Reframe Grid

Most professionals believe their thoughts are facts. But they're often just perceptions filtered through old experiences. Here's a 3-step mental check-in:

Situation	Thought	Emotion	Reframe
A client rejected my proposal	"I'm not good enough."	Embarrassed	"It was one pitch. I'm still growing and improving."

Use this format during weekly reflections or journaling. Over time, it helps ***rephrase negative beliefs*** *and rewires emotional patterns.*

Tool 3: "Zoom Out" Regulation Strategy

Imagine you're zooming out from your problem—like viewing it from 30,000 feet. This strategy also encourages **adopting a realistic and optimistic perspective.**

Ask:

- Will this matter 5 days from now?
- Will it still bother me in 5 months?
- What would my wiser future self say?

Use when: Trapped in overthinking or emotional spirals during high-stakes moments at work.

Coaching Prompt: "Am I reacting from this moment—or responding from my mission?"

Tool 4: The 90-Second Rule

Neuroscientist Dr. Jill Bolte Taylor found that the biochemical lifespan of an emotion is only 90 seconds. If it lasts longer, we are feeding it with thought loops. **Engaging in mindfulness practices like deep breathing exercises can help regulate stress and reduce anxiety within this timeframe.**

Try this:

- When upset, look at a timer and breathe deeply for 90 seconds.
- Let the emotion rise and fall—like a wave.
- Don't fuel it with stories. Just breathe.

This is the emotional version of letting a wave pass without drowning in it.

Tool 5: Emotional Reset Box

Create a physical or digital "reset box" filled with tools that regulate your nervous system. These can be part of your broader **stress management techniques**:

- A calming playlist
- 3 gratitude screenshots
- A quote that always grounds you
- A picture of someone you love
- A 5-min guided breathing video
- *Consider also including a reminder for a quick physical activity, a journaling prompt, or a link to a brief guided meditation.*

Keep it ready on your phone or work desk for high-stress moments.

5.5 Emotional Granularity – Becoming Fluent in Your Feelings

Most professionals use just a handful of emotional words—happy, stressed, tired, fine. But emotional granularity is the ability to distinguish between similar emotions with precision, like telling the difference between irritated, disappointed, and dismissed. This precision is also key to **healthy emotional expression** and helps you **overcome negative thoughts and emotions**.

Why it matters: According to research by Dr. Lisa Feldman Barrett, individuals with high emotional granularity are:

- Better at handling stress
- Less likely to emotionally "explode" at small triggers
- More adaptable in high-stakes environments

The Upgrade: Instead of saying:

- "I'm stressed," try: "I'm feeling under-prepared and a bit vulnerable."
- "I'm angry," try: "I feel unacknowledged and excluded."

Benefit for busy professionals: The more precise your vocabulary, the more precise your response. You become less reactive, more strategic.

Coaching Prompt: "Can I go one level deeper and name the real emotion here?"

5.6 Respond, Don't React – The Emotional Power Gap

In high-speed professional life, the biggest wins often come from emotional pauses. Reacting is impulsive. Responding is intentional. This applies not only to internal states but also when **dealing with difficult people**.

Reacting

- Triggered by old stories or unprocessed fear
- Often regretted
- Automatic

Responding

- Anchored in values and goals
- Considered
- Calm under pressure

Example: A client emails a harsh complaint.

- **Reaction:** "I will shoot back a defensive reply."
- **Response:** "I will acknowledge their frustration and propose a solution after a 10-minute breather."

Tool: The 3-Breath Rule

Before replying to any difficult message:

- Inhale for 4 counts
- Hold for 2
- Exhale slowly for 6

Now respond.

This 12-second gap is your power to lead with composure, even in challenging interpersonal interactions.

5.7 Key Learnings + Quick Actionables

Built especially for the fast-moving, high-achieving, emotionally overloaded world of today's professionals.

Key Learnings

- **Emotional mastery isn't suppression—it's skilled self-leadership.** Busy professionals don't have the luxury to "lose it"—but they also don't need to bottle it. Mastery means noticing, naming, and navigating emotions with intelligence.
- **Moods and emotions are not the same.** A bad 2 minutes doesn't have to become a bad day. Learning to pause, zoom out, and choose a wiser response is a learnable skill.
- **Labeling emotions reduces their grip.** The more nuanced your emotional vocabulary, the more equipped you are to handle the storm. Emotional granularity builds both empathy and effectiveness.
- **Your greatest leverage point is the gap between stimulus and response.** It's not what happens—it's how you handle what happens. And that power lies in the pause.
- **Self-compassion is a crucial tactic for increasing emotional resilience** and moving from self-criticism to self-acceptance when facing challenges.
- **Proactively managing stress, coping with setbacks, and dealing with difficult people** are integrated parts of achieving inner peace and sustainable happiness.
- **Building a robust support system and knowing when to seek professional assistance** are vital for long-term emotional well-being.

Quick Actionables for Busy Professionals

Action	Frequency	Time Needed	Purpose
Label your emotion out loud (name it)	Daily	30 sec	Activates calm thinking, disarms emotional hijack
Practice a self-compassion moment (e.g., a kind thought to yourself)	Daily	1 min	Boosts emotional resilience and self-acceptance
Use the 3-Breath Rule before replying to difficult emails	As needed	12 sec	Turns reaction into response
Start a Mood Tracker (emoji log or app)	Daily	1 min	Spot patterns in emotional energy
Weekly Reframe Journal – 1 moment you reacted, 1 you rewired	Weekly	10 min	Builds self-awareness and inner growth
Create your Reset Box (playlist, images, quotes)	One-time setup	15–20 min	Easy access to emotional regulation tools
Practice "Zoom Out" thinking on setbacks	As needed	2–5 min	Builds emotional maturity and wisdom, promotes growth mindset
Learn 5 new emotional words this week	Weekly	5 min	Expands your emotional granularity
Schedule 1 Emotionally Honest Conversation (personal or professional)	Bi-weekly	30 min	Strengthens connection + self-leadership; builds social support
Engage in a brief stress management technique (e.g., short walk, focused breathing)	Daily	5-10 min	Proactively reduces stress and clears mind
Reflect on a setback with a "What can I learn?" mindset	As needed	5 min	Fosters a growth mindset and future planning
Identify one strategy to handle a specific difficult interaction	As needed	2 min	Prepares for challenging social dynamics

(e.g., "stay calm," "discuss privately")			
Research options for professional mental health support (optional, for future reference)	One-time	10 min	Builds a resource for deeper challenges

Coaching Reminder: "You cannot lead others until you can calmly lead yourself."

5.8 Additional Resources

(Useful for deeper study or as self-practice links for readers to explore when they need)

Topic	Suggested Resource	Type
Emotional granularity	How Emotions Are Made – Dr. Lisa Feldman Barrett	Book
Emotional regulation science	The Science of Emotion – Yale Center for Emotional Intelligence	Website
Mood tracking	Daylio App	Mobile App
Mindful pausing	Headspace: Emotional Agility Series	Guided Audio
Emotional labeling practice	The Feelings Wheel by Dr. Gloria Willcox	Visual Tool
Workplace well-being	Harvard Business Review: Emotional Intelligence	Articles Collection

Chapter 6:
Relationships – The Happiness Multiplier

6.1 The Science of Social Connection and Happiness

Why investing in people around you multiplies your inner joy!

> *"Connection is why we're here. It's what gives purpose and meaning to our lives."*
>
> — Dr. Brené Brown

Why it Matters

As busy professionals, we often prioritize performance over presence. Emails over eye contact. Deadlines over dinner dates. But science tells us that while achievement fuels success, genuine connection sustains happiness and builds resilience. It's in our interactions, both personal and professional, that we find a deeper sense of fulfillment.

Landmark Research: The Harvard Study of Adult Development

Started in 1938, this study followed two groups of men for over 80 years—one from Harvard, the other from low-income Boston neighborhoods. The goal was simple: What makes people truly thrive?

> **Finding:** *"The clearest predictor of a happy and long life wasn't wealth, fame, or achievement. It was the quality of their relationships."*
>
> — Robert Waldinger, MD, Study Director

Those with warm relationships:

- Lived longer
- Fell ill less often
- Recovered faster from stress
- Retained sharper cognitive function in later years

Even at age 50, it wasn't cholesterol or career level that predicted health at 80—it was satisfaction in their relationships.

6.2 What Happens in the Brain?

Social connection isn't just emotionally comforting—it's biologically essential.

- **Oxytocin Boosts Trust and Bonding**
    - Released during touch, kindness, eye contact, and shared joy
    - Lowers cortisol (stress hormone), reduces anxiety
    - Builds empathy and connection—even in short conversations
- **Dopamine = Joy through Shared Moments**
    - Celebrating small wins with others creates dopamine spikes
    - Laughter, collaboration, affection: all natural dopamine boosters
- **Social Rejection Triggers Pain Centers**
    - Studies show that social exclusion activates the same brain regions as physical pain
    - Loneliness isn't just a feeling—it's a health risk

What the Numbers Say:

- People with strong social ties are 50% more likely to survive over time compared to those who are isolated (Holt-Lunstad, Brigham Young University).
- Married people, on average, live longer and report higher happiness—when the relationship is warm and supportive.
- Quality > quantity. Having one or two deeply trusted connections is far more powerful than hundreds of surface-level ones.

Connection in the Modern Workplace

In hybrid work and high-demand environments, many professionals report "performing with people, not connecting with them." But emotional isolation at work:

- Lowers engagement
- Increases burnout risk
- Erodes creativity and trust

Building positive work relationships, characterized by effective communication and mutual support, is crucial for a happy work environment and career success. Creating micro-moments of connection (a "How are you—really?", 5 minutes of undivided presence, recognition in a team call) can dramatically uplift emotional energy.

Coaching Reflection:

"Where in my day do I show up with people instead of just through them?"

6.3 How Relationships Impact Stress, Longevity, and Joy

"When we are seen, heard, and valued—we heal. And when we offer that to others, we grow."

Relationships are not just emotionally comforting—they are biologically protective. The presence (or absence) of meaningful relationships shapes how we experience stress, how our body responds to challenges, and how much joy we feel on a day-to-day basis. **A sense of purpose in your work can also contribute to reduced stress and greater resilience, positively influencing your interactions.**

Stress Buffering Effect

When you feel emotionally safe with someone—a friend, mentor, spouse, or colleague—your nervous system registers this safety. That's why venting to a close friend, even without solving the problem, brings relief.

- Physiological proof: Holding a loved one's hand lowers blood pressure and heart rate during stressful events (Coan et al., 2006).
- Verbal reassurance activates the prefrontal cortex and reduces amygdala activity—calming the fear response.

Coaching Insight:

"Sometimes you don't need a solution—you need a witness."

Longevity and Health

Strong relationships are as important to physical health as diet, exercise, or sleep. Cultivating a strong social support system, including family and friends, provides a network that extends beyond the work environment, crucial for overall well-being.

- In a review of 148 studies (over 300,000 people), social connection was found to improve chances of survival by 50%.
- Lonely individuals have higher rates of inflammation, hypertension, and compromised immunity.

Fact: Chronic loneliness is now considered more dangerous than obesity and comparable to smoking 15 cigarettes a day (Holt-Lunstad, 2010).

The connection is clear: The more meaningfully connected you are, the more resilient your body becomes.

Joy Amplifier

Joy isn't just created—it's shared.

Think about:

- The laughter you couldn't stop during lunch with a colleague
- The deep calm after talking to your best friend
- The pride you felt when your team appreciated your effort

These are micro-moments of shared joy. They create emotional memory, strengthen bonds, and build your emotional reserves for harder days.

Neuroscience insight: Celebrating wins with others triggers stronger dopamine responses than celebrating alone.

Summary: Why This Matters to Busy Professionals

For leaders, changemakers, and corporate high performers, relationship-building often takes a back seat. But ignoring relationships isn't a time-saver—it's a well-being tax.

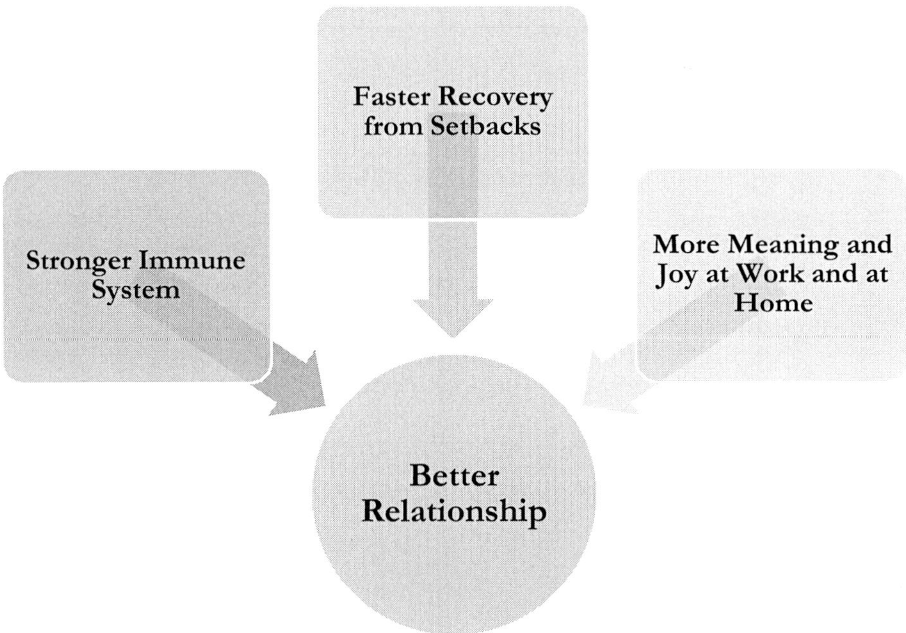

Coaching Reflection:

"Who do I feel most myself around—and how often am I prioritizing time with them?"

6.4 The Types of Relationships That Matter Most (Especially for Busy Professionals)

Not all connections feed our soul—or our success. In today's high-speed world, busy professionals often engage in hundreds of interactions weekly, yet still feel emotionally undernourished. That's because what matters isn't the quantity of connections—it's their quality and function. **Maintaining positive relationships in your network can lead to fresh professional prospects and valuable guidance.**

Here's a practical guide to the five core types of relationships that deeply influence happiness, health, and professional well-being.

1. The Anchor (Emotional Safety Net)

This is the person you can truly be yourself with. They ground you, listen without fixing, and reflect your worth even when you can't see it yourself.

- Example: A spouse, a long-time friend, a coach, or even a mentor who just "gets you."
- Why it matters: Emotional safety reduces stress, supports mental health, and enhances emotional regulation.

Coaching Prompt: "When things go wrong, who do I call first—not to solve it, but just to sit with it?"

2. The Mirror (Growth Partner)

This person challenges your assumptions and reflects blind spots. They don't just agree with you—they grow with you.

- Example: A trusted colleague, mentor, or coach who gives honest feedback.
- Why it matters: Encourages self-awareness, humility, and consistent personal development.

Watch out for: Always surrounding yourself with "yes-people." Growth needs friction.

3. The Believer (Confidence Amplifier)

This person sees your potential even when you're doubting yourself. They remind you of who you are and why your work matters.

- Example: A past teacher, inspiring friend, or even a younger mentee who looks up to you.
- Why it matters: Boosts self-confidence, motivation, and resilience.

Neuroscience: Social encouragement activates the brain's reward system more than self-affirmation alone.

4. The Peer Circle (Relatability + Relief)

A small group of peers who understand your world. They may not be your best friends—but they know the pressures you face.

- Example: Fellow leaders, startup founders, corporate peers, or mastermind group.
- Why it matters: Helps normalize stress, reduce isolation, and exchange wisdom. You realize you're not alone.

Pro Tip: Create or join a "CEO Coffee Circle" or "Thursday Leadership Huddle."

5. The Uplifted Stranger (Micro-Moments of Joy)

Not all happiness comes from deep relationships. Sometimes, a smile from a stranger, Chaiwala's kind word, chat with your Office Boy, or a short elevator chat with a security guard of your building can shift your energy.

- Example: Uber driver, vegetable vendor, Ramu kaka, grocery cashier, someone you exchange a joke with.
- Why it matters: These brief but warm interactions increase oxytocin and remind us we're part of a shared human experience.

Coaching Insight: "Never underestimate the power of a 90-second conversation."

Why This Categorization Matters

Busy professionals often prioritize networking—but overlook nourishing. Knowing the roles that people play in your emotional ecosystem helps:

- Invest wisely: Who do you need more of in your life?
- Set boundaries: Who is draining but not serving any role?
- Curate connection intentionally instead of defaulting to what's convenient.

Reflection Question:

"What type of connection am I missing most right now—and how can I seek it intentionally?"

6.5 Navigating Difficult People and Relationship Drains

How to protect your peace and energy when time is limited!

> *"You don't have to attend every argument you're invited to."*
> — Anonymous

In the high-stakes life of a busy professional, time is scarce—but emotional bandwidth is even scarcer. And nothing drains that bandwidth faster than difficult, energy-sapping relationships. Whether it's a combative coworker, a passive-aggressive manager, or a draining relative, learning to manage these dynamics gracefully is a core happiness skill.

Understanding Emotional Drain

Not all difficult people are toxic. But when interactions become repetitively energy-depleting, they erode your focus, clarity, and happiness.

Common energy-draining traits:

- Chronic negativity or complaining
- Drama or constant urgency
- Passive aggression or guilt-tripping
- Inability to respect boundaries
- Taking but never giving (emotionally or practically)

Coaching Insight:

"You may not be able to change them—but you can change the energy exchange."

Tools for Navigating Draining Relationships

1. Set Clear Boundaries (Without Guilt)

"I'm happy to help, but I need 24 hours to respond."

"Let's agree to focus this conversation on solutions, not just problems."

"I don't have capacity for this right now. Can we revisit it next week?"

Why this works: Boundaries aren't rejection—they're protection. For them and for you. **Understanding company guidelines and the distinction between professional and personal relationships can further aid in setting appropriate boundaries.**

2. Use the "Energy Audit" Technique

At the end of your day, reflect:

- Who gave me energy?
- Who drained it?
- Who did I give too much of myself to today?

Track this for a week. You'll quickly identify patterns—and relationships that need recalibration.

3. Shift from Reacting to Responding

When someone triggers you, pause. Take one breath. Ask yourself:

"What's this really about?"

"Is this about me—or something unresolved in them?"

This creates emotional distance—so you don't hand over your peace in the heat of the moment. **This also aligns with the advice to examine your own reaction when offended and to stay calm.**

4. The "3-Fence Rule"

Not everyone deserves equal emotional access.

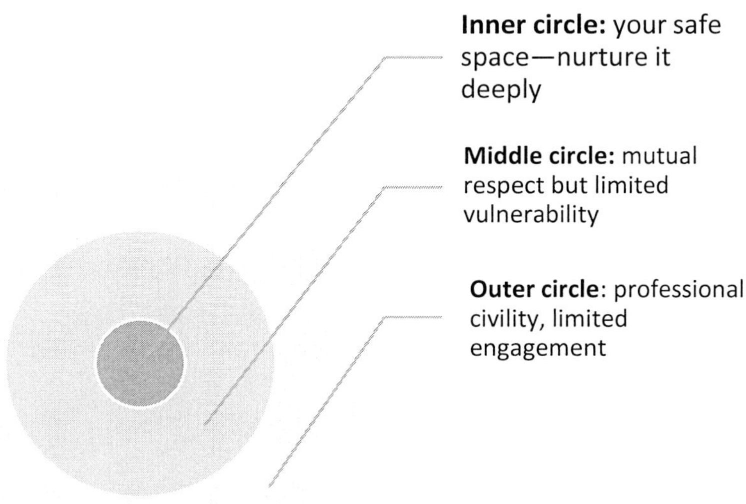

Assigning people to appropriate "fences" helps you avoid emotional overload. **It's also important to avoid engaging in gossip, as it undermines trust and a healthy work environment.**

5. Master the Art of Graceful Exit

You don't owe anyone extended emotional labor when it becomes harmful.

Try these:

- "I hear you, and I'd like to reflect on this—can we pause here?"
- "Let's continue this when we're both in a better headspace."
- "This doesn't feel productive right now. I'm going to step away."

Busy Professional Tip: Keep a go-to sentence in your back pocket for draining moments. Practice it. **When problems arise with colleagues, try to have a kind and sincere discussion privately first.**

6. Reinvest That Energy Elsewhere

Every minute spent managing toxic dynamics is a minute stolen from:

- Your passions
- Your well-being
- Your people who lift you up

Instead of ruminating, redirect. Go for a walk. Text someone you love. Do one tiny act that feeds you. **Remember to remain positive in interactions and support fellow team members by focusing on their successes.**

Reflection Prompt:

"What is this relationship costing me—and what do I need to reclaim?"

6.6 Rituals to Deepen Relationships (Even in a Busy Schedule)

Connection doesn't require more time—just more intention.

> *"Love grows in attention, not duration."*
> — Dr. Mandeep Sharma

In the rush of modern professional life, most people say:

"I wish I had more time for my people."

But the truth is—you don't need more hours; you need better rituals. Small, consistent habits of connection go further than grand gestures. **These rituals are key to building positive working relationships and maintaining a healthy network.**

Below are relationship rituals specifically designed for busy professionals to nurture personal and work bonds, even with limited time and energy.

1. The "Five-Minute Favor"

Once a day, do one tiny thing to make someone's life easier:

- Forward a useful article to a mentee
- Share praise for a colleague on a team chat
- Call your parent while walking between meetings

Why it works: Acts of service deepen bonds—and require no scheduling. **This embodies the spirit of supporting fellow team members and building goodwill.**

2. One-Sentence Appreciation Ritual

Every Friday, send one short message to someone you appreciate:

"Hey, I really appreciated your calm presence this week."

"Just wanted to say—you inspire me."

Format: SMS, email, Slack, handwritten note. Doesn't matter. What matters is consistency.

Why it works: It strengthens the connection—and rewires your brain to notice the good.

3. 2-Minute Full Presence Rule

In your next interaction—at home or work—pause everything else.

Look them in the eye.

Put away the phone.

Say: "I'm here. What's up?"

Even 2 minutes of full presence builds trust more than 30 distracted ones. **This is a core aspect of effective communication, which entails both speaking and active listening, and paying attention to nonverbal cues.**

For parents: Apply this when you return home. Those first two minutes are gold.

4. Monthly 1:1 Personal Check-ins (Non-Work)

Set a recurring 30-minute call or coffee with:

- Your collegue or manager—but don't talk work
- A sibling or parent
- A mentee or old friend

Prompt to Start:

"How's your energy been lately? What's been bringing you joy or stress?"

Put it in your calendar. Protect it like a meeting with your CEO.

5. Shared Rituals of Joy

Have a short ritual with someone close:

- Tuesday coffee with your partner
- "Friday Memes" exchange with your best friend
- Monthly hike or movie with your sibling

Why it works: Rituals anchor relationships in time, tradition, and meaning—even when everything else feels chaotic.

6. Mini Reconnection After Conflict

After a disagreement, don't wait days for things to simmer. Use a short script like:

"We don't have to solve it now, but I care about us. Can we circle back later?"

"I may have reacted fast. I want to understand better."

This ritual of reconnection prevents emotional distancing from becoming permanent disconnection. **It demonstrates consistency and a commitment to trust in the relationship.**

Coaching Insight for Busy Professionals:

"In your calendar this week, who gets your full attention—not just your time?"

6.7 My Coaching Prompts to Strengthen Key Relationships

For busy professionals seeking meaningful connection—without adding to their to-do list

> *"The quality of your relationships determines the quality of your life. The best way to deepen a relationship? Ask better, meaningful questions & stay curious."*
>
> — Dr. Mandeep Sharma

For time-starved professionals, it's not about more conversations. It's about more meaningful ones.

When time is tight, we often fall into functional interactions:

"Did you send the report?"

"What's for dinner?"

"Did you pick up the groceries?"

These keep life running. But they don't grow connection.

What deepens relationships is curiosity, presence, and a few well-placed questions.

The Relationship Reset: One Powerful Question at a Time

Below are targeted coaching-style prompts—each designed to unlock insight, empathy, and connection.

Use one per day, per week, or per month. Use them at home, in your team, or with old friends.

Prompts for Family and Close Relationships

- "What's been the most stressful part of your week?"

  (Creates a space to unload, not just perform.)
- "What can I do to support you better right now?"

  (Shows humility and commitment without guessing.)
- "What's one small thing that's made you smile lately?"

  (Builds positivity bias and shared joy.)
- "If you had a 3-day reset, what would you do with it?"

  (Uncovers desires they may have buried under duty.)

Prompts for Colleagues and Work Peers

- "Where are you feeling stretched right now?"

  (Opens a door to vulnerability in high-performance teams.)
- "What's one thing you're proud of that no one noticed?"

  (Affirms effort, not just outcome.)
- "What part of your work gives you energy vs. drains it?"

  (Leads to better role alignment and support.)
- "If you could redesign one part of your workday, what would it be?"

  (Invites innovation, autonomy, and empathy.)

Prompts for Reconnecting with Old Friends

- "What's something you've learned about yourself this year?"
- "When do you feel most like you these days?"
- "What's one thing we used to do that you miss?"
- "If we had 24 hours together, no limits—what would we do?"

These reignite shared history with forward-facing connection.

Prompts for Self-Reflection About Relationships

Even with limited time, a single question can help you reclaim emotional clarity. Try journaling or reflecting on:

- "Who energizes me after I talk to them? Who depletes me?"
- "Where have I not said what I truly feel—out of fear?"
- "What relationship do I want to heal this year?"
- "Who do I miss—but haven't told?"

Coaching Insight:

"Even five intentional minutes can heal months of silence."

6.8 Key Learnings + Quick Actionables

Because time is short—and connection matters more than ever

Key Learnings

- **Strong relationships are the #1 predictor of long-term happiness.** According to Harvard's 85-year longitudinal study, quality of relationships—not wealth, fame, or work success—is the biggest contributor to a joyful and long life.
- **Emotional nourishment > time spent.** A short, sincere connection (even 2 minutes of full attention) can deepen bonds more than hours of distracted presence.
- **Relationships protect your health.** Social connection improves immunity, reduces stress, lowers risk of chronic disease, and increases life expectancy. **Additionally, a good work-life balance is crucial, as neglected personal life and constant overwork can lead to strained relationships and burnout.**
- **Toxic relationships cost more than time—they cost energy.** Learning to set emotional boundaries and practicing graceful exits is not selfish—it's essential. **This includes recognizing the importance of communication, trustworthiness, and positive interactions.**
- **Relationship rituals make happiness sustainable.** Tiny, repeatable actions like a Friday appreciation message or a monthly check-in build joy without needing major schedule overhauls.

Quick Actionables for Busy Professionals

Time	Action	Category
2 min	Send one message of appreciation to a colleague or loved one	Micro-connection
5 min	Ask: "What was the most stressful part of your week?" to your partner or child	Emotional presence
10 min	Do an "Energy Audit" – Who gave you energy today? Who drained it?	Emotional clarity
Weekly	Schedule one "non-work" 1:1 check-in with a friend or team member	Relationship health
Monthly	Host a 30-min virtual coffee or walk with someone you miss	Social renewal
Post-conflict	Use a reconnection phrase: "I care about us—can we revisit this later?"	Conflict repair
Every Sunday	Review your calendar: "Who gets my time? Who needs my attention?"	Intentional alignment
Daily	**Practice active listening and empathy in conversations.**	Communication
As needed	**Privately address workplace issues with colleagues.**	Conflict resolution
Weekly	**Plan brief activities outside of work to foster personal ties.**	Work-life balance

Recommended Resources for High Impact, Low Time

- Harvard Study on Adult Development - Harvard Gazette Summary
- "The Art of Gathering" by Priya Parker: Brilliant for designing better connection moments—even in meetings.
- The Gottman Institute Tools (for couples & professional conflict)
- "Radical Candor" Framework by Kim Scott (for building trust at work)
- The "6-Minute Networker" Technique by Joe Apfelbaum: Free LinkedIn-focused guide

Final Coaching Prompt:

"If your time is your most precious asset, who are the people worth investing it in—deeply, consistently, intentionally?"

Chapter 7:
Role of Life – Purpose in Happiness

7.1 The Role of Purpose and Meaning

Why Knowing Your "Why" Makes Every Hour Count for Busy Professionals!

> *"When work drains you, purpose sustains you."*
> — Dr. Mandeep Sharma

For the busy professional, time is the rarest currency. You can't afford to waste it on things that feel hollow. That's why the pursuit of purpose isn't a luxury—it's a lifeline.

When your work aligns with meaning, it fuels energy rather than depleting it. When your actions reflect your values, your days feel whole—not just full. **Cultivating an attitude of gratitude can further amplify this sense of fulfillment, helping you appreciate the meaningful aspects of your life and work.**

7.2 Why Meaning Matters More Than Ever

Research Snapshot:

A 2019 study in JAMA Network Open found that people with a strong sense of purpose had lower mortality risk, better sleep, and fewer chronic diseases—even after controlling for income and education.

But it's not just about living longer. It's about living better.

For professionals constantly toggling between meetings, emails, and deadlines, a deep sense of purpose:

- Anchors you in your values, not your to-do list
- Helps you say no without guilt
- Turns routine tasks into meaningful contributions
- Prevents burnout by giving pain a reason

This commitment to purpose also supports a holistic approach to well-being, nurturing greater physical and mental health.

> *"Purpose doesn't make hard days disappear.*
> *It makes them worth it."*
>
> — Dr. Mandeep Sharma

7.3 What is Purpose (Really)?

Clarity for the Time-Strapped, Meaning-Seeking Professional

"Purpose is not a job title. It's a reason to show up, even when no one's watching."

Many busy professionals mistakenly equate purpose with profession. But your purpose isn't what you do. It's why you do it. It's the inner compass that guides decisions, fuels motivation, and infuses each action—big or small—with meaning. It's that quiet conviction: "This matters. I matter."

Defining Purpose in Plain Language

Purpose = Contribution + Meaning + Consistency

Element	What It Means
Contribution	You feel your work or actions help others or add value
Meaning	It connects with your personal beliefs, values, or sense of mission
Consistency	You return to it regularly—it becomes a thread through your life and choices

Snapshot: Two Professionals, Two Paths

1. **Same job, different outcomes:**

   A product manager may feel drained and robotic—checking tickets, running sprints. Another, in the same role, feels deeply fulfilled—seeing how each release improves customer lives.

   The difference? One sees tasks. The other sees purpose.

2. **Same output, different intention:**

   A doctor who saves lives but is burned out vs. one who has rediscovered meaning in healing—not just curing. A parent working 14-hour days who feels guilt vs. one who sees those hours as building legacy and possibility for their child.

   Purpose isn't about changing your life. It's about changing your lens.

Coaching Reflection:

"If everything on your calendar disappeared tomorrow, what would you still choose to do—and why?"

That question often holds the seeds of purpose.

Here's a simple, powerful tool tailored for busy professionals to uncover their purpose without needing hours of reflection:

Tool: "The 5-Minute Purpose Discovery Map"

A guided, bite-sized exercise to clarify your WHY—even with a packed calendar.

Time required: 5 minutes

Best time: During a break, commute, or end-of-day reflection

Step 1: The Energy Audit

Think about the last 3 days. Write down:

- 1 activity that made you feel energized or proud
- 1 task that felt draining or hollow

Prompt:

What about that energizing task gave you meaning? What was missing from the draining one?

Step 2: The "Impact Scan"

Ask:

- Who do I most enjoy helping?
- What kind of problems do I instinctively want to solve?
- Where do I feel I have made a real difference, even in small ways?

Highlight the type of contribution that keeps showing up.

Step 3: The Values Check

Circle the 3 values that matter most to you from this shortlist:

- Growth
- Connection
- Integrity
- Impact
- Creativity
- Freedom
- Contribution
- Spirituality
- Curiosity
- Joy

Now ask: How well does my current day-to-day reflect these values?

Step 4: Your "Purpose Statement Lite"

Fill in the blanks:

I feel most alive when I'm helping _______ to ________, in a way that reflects my value of ________.

Examples:

- I feel most alive when I'm helping teams simplify problems, in a way that reflects my value of clarity.
- I feel most alive when I'm helping young leaders grow, in a way that reflects my value of contribution.

Keep this as a post-it on your laptop, your phone lock screen, or journal cover.

In addition, here's a more reflective, high-impact purpose discovery tool for all professionals—not just busy ones—who seek to uncover deeper meaning in life, with happiness as the outcome.

Tool: The IKIGAI-Inspired Purpose Compass for Happiness

A step-by-step tool to align your life with what truly matters

Inspired by the Japanese concept of Ikigai, this tool guides individuals to find the intersection of joy, skill, service, and meaning—with happiness as the true destination.

Step 1: Passion Reflection — What brings you joy?

Ask yourself:

- What activities make you lose track of time?
- When was the last time you felt truly alive or playful?
- What would you do if money were not a factor?

Write 3–5 things you absolutely enjoy doing—even if you don't get paid for them.

Step 2: Strength Scan — What are you naturally good at?

Prompt:

- What do people often come to you for?
- What have you been praised or recognized for in your work or life?

List 3–5 strengths or talents (e.g., explaining ideas, listening, designing, leading).

Step 3: Impact Check — What does the world need?

Think beyond careers:

- What problems do you wish were solved in your community or workplace?
- Whose suffering or struggle do you deeply empathize with?

Note 2–3 causes or needs that resonate with your heart.

Step 4: Contribution Reality — What can you be paid or valued for?

Don't just think job roles. Think value creation.

- What can you do that helps others win?
- Where does your skill meet someone's need?

Write down 2–3 ways you already—or could—create meaningful value.

Now Connect the Dots:

Draw four overlapping circles labeled:

- What I Love
- What I'm Good At
- What the World Needs
- What I Can Be Valued For

Where all four circles meet lies your Purpose Zone—a unique alignment that leads not just to success, but to deep happiness.

Final Reflection:

"What's one small shift I can make this week to move closer to that zone?"

This could be:

- Volunteering 1 hour doing something meaningful
- Having one deep conversation about your passions
- Delegating a draining task to focus on work that fulfills you

7.4 Purpose and the Science of Happiness

Why having a "why" matters more than ever, especially for busy professionals?

In our pursuit of happiness, one of the most powerful—yet often overlooked—ingredients is purpose. While material success, leisure, or social connections can bring momentary joy, lasting happiness and resilience often stem from feeling that our life matters, that we're contributing to something greater than ourselves.

What Science Says About Purpose and Well-being

Psychological studies have consistently shown that people who live with a sense of purpose report higher levels of well-being, lower rates of depression, and even longer lives. A major longitudinal study published in Psychological Science followed over 6,000 individuals for 14 years and found that those with a strong sense of purpose had a 15% lower risk of death, regardless of age, wealth, or health.

Another study from *JAMA Psychiatry* discovered that people with high purpose scores had better sleep, stronger immune systems, and more consistent emotional regulation—even when faced with setbacks. Purpose seems to act like a psychological buffer, helping people recover from challenges with greater ease and maintain emotional equilibrium. **This resilience is also supported by embracing challenges as opportunities for growth, rather than insurmountable obstacles.**

Why Purpose Matters More for Busy Professionals

For professionals juggling packed calendars, endless emails, and competing demands, purpose becomes more than a lofty ideal—it becomes a grounding force.

Without clarity of purpose, it's easy to fall into the trap of:

- Feeling like you're just "going through the motions"
- Constantly checking boxes but never feeling fulfilled
- Measuring success by external metrics rather than internal alignment

Purpose also encourages prioritizing self-care—including adequate sleep, a healthy diet, and regular exercise—all crucial for sustaining your energy and focus.

When you reconnect with your purpose, even the busiest schedules feel more meaningful. Purpose turns routine into ritual. It turns burnout into contribution. It gives context to every decision.

How Purpose Rewires Your Brain

Neuroscientific research shows that a strong sense of purpose activates the ventromedial prefrontal cortex, a brain region associated with meaning, value, and future planning. This activation leads to:

- Improved goal persistence
- Stronger emotional regulation
- Reduced stress response

In simple terms: purposeful people bounce back faster, focus longer, and stay emotionally steadier—even under pressure.

Coaching Insight:

"You don't need to quit your job to live your purpose. You need to bring your purpose into how you show up at your job."

Whether you're a doctor, consultant, manager, or entrepreneur, your why can infuse everyday actions with deeper satisfaction.

Scientific Findings on Purpose and Happiness

Study / Source	Key Finding	Implication for Busy Professionals
Psychological Science (2014)	Purposeful individuals had 15% lower mortality risk over 14 years	Having a clear purpose adds resilience and longevity
JAMA Psychiatry (2020)	Purpose correlated with better sleep, stronger immunity, emotional regulation	Even under pressure, purpose helps the body & mind recover better
American Journal of Epidemiology (2009)	Purpose linked with reduced risk of stroke, heart attack, and depression	Aligning daily work with personal values supports health
Stanford Center on Longevity	Purpose-driven people show higher physical function in aging	Purpose safeguards vitality during high-demand career phases
Harvard Grant Study	Meaningful relationships & purpose predict long-term happiness more than income or fame	Purpose drives deeper fulfillment beyond titles and salary
Dr. Martin Seligman – Positive Psychology	Purpose is one of the five core elements of well-being (PERMA model)	Building purpose boosts overall life satisfaction and work engagement

7.5 Examples & Stories of Busy Professionals Who Found Meaning

Proof that purpose isn't just a theory—it's a life-shifting reality.

In this section, we bring to life the abstract idea of "purpose" through real stories of professionals who discovered deeper meaning within, or beyond, their careers. These aren't superhumans—they're people like you: juggling responsibilities, fighting burnout, and craving something more.

1. **The Consultant Who Found Purpose in Mentorship**

   Rajiv, a senior consultant in a global IT firm, was once hyper-focused on promotions, KPIs, and client metrics. He was successful—but exhausted. During a leadership offsite, he was asked: "What do you wish someone had told you 10 years ago?"

   That one question led him to start informally mentoring younger associates over coffee. Within a year, he'd created a "Peer Lift Circle" at his company. His evenings went from draining to energizing. He says:

   "I finally felt like I was building something that mattered beyond deadlines."

   Reflection: Purpose doesn't require a career change. Sometimes it's about adding meaning to the job you already do.

2. **The Corporate Lawyer Who Became a Wellness Advocate**

   Meera, a partner at a prestigious law firm, spent 12 years scaling the ladder. But a stress-induced health scare forced a pause. In her recovery, she began studying mindfulness and nutrition—not for others, but for herself.

   A year later, she launched "Well Counsel," a wellness initiative for women in legal careers. Her purpose emerged not from her achievements, but her pain.

   "My burnout became the bridge to helping others avoid the same path."

   Reflection: Sometimes purpose is born from the very struggle you once resented.

3. **The Startup CEO Who Reconnected with His Childhood Passion**

   Arun, a 38-year-old startup founder, had lost his spark. Despite funding, traction, and press, he felt empty. During a sabbatical, he revisited a childhood passion—visual storytelling.

He began volunteering at weekends to teach underprivileged kids in Noida how to animate short videos for social media. Over time, this small act became a big mission: his company now sponsors creative tech programs in semi-rural schools of Uttar Pradesh in India.

"Reconnecting with that playful part of me reignited my mission."

Reflection: Your inner child often holds the seeds of your most authentic purpose.

4. **The Doctor Who Turned System Fatigue Into System Change**

   Dr. Kavitha, a busy hospital physician at Bangalore India, was frustrated by the gaps in patient communication and aftercare. She started by creating simple visual leaflets for her department to explain procedures better.

   Three years later, she's the founder of a health-tech platform improving patient literacy across India.

   "I wanted to change the system from within. My stethoscope became my mic."

   Reflection: Purpose often whispers in the small frustrations. Listen closely.

Coaching Prompt for Readers:

"If your calendar looks full but your heart feels empty, where might your deeper 'why' be hiding?"

7.6 Reflective Prompts for Busy Professionals

Designed to help busy professionals discover meaning, even in the middle of packed schedules.

In the hustle of everyday responsibilities, taking even 10 minutes to reflect can feel like a luxury. But these carefully crafted tools are built for high-impact clarity in minimal time. They are not meant to add pressure, but to offer perspective.

Worksheet 1: The 5-Minute Purpose Reflection

Use this when you're short on time but need a reset.

Prompt	Your Response
What am I doing today that feels meaningful to me?	
When was the last time I felt deeply fulfilled? What was I doing?	
Who do I want to positively impact today—even in a small way?	
What would I still love to be doing 10 years from now?	
If today were the last page of a chapter, what title would I give it?	

Tip: Revisit this once a week—track patterns, and listen to what lights you up.

Worksheet 2: Purpose Audit – The Alignment Check

Designed for professionals managing multiple roles.

Area of Life	How Aligned Do You Feel? (1–5)	What Would Make This More Purposeful?
Work (daily tasks)		
Career Direction		
Health & Well-being		
Family / Relationships		
Hobbies / Creative Outlets		
Contribution to Society		

Coaching Insight: When even one area feels aligned, it becomes easier to bring that energy into others.

Prompt Cards for Inner Clarity

Use any of these as journal entries, team openers, or coffee break reflections:

- "If I couldn't fail, how would I show up differently?"
- "What's one story I want to be remembered for?"
- "What's something I have postponed that might actually bring joy?"
- "If my younger self met me today, what would they admire?"
- "Who do I admire, and what does that tell me about my values?"

7.7 Key Learnings + Quick Actionables

Because transformation only happens when insight meets action.

Key Learnings

- Purpose is not a luxury—it's a necessity for emotional resilience and long-term happiness. Research proves that a sense of meaning reduces stress, boosts health, and improves decision-making—especially under pressure.
- You don't have to quit your job to find purpose. Many professionals uncover deeper fulfillment by reframing how they work, mentoring others, or aligning tasks with personal values.
- Purpose evolves over time. What drives you today may shift. The key is to remain in conversation with your inner self—through journaling, coaching, or mindful reflection.
- Meaning protects against burnout. Busy professionals who feel connected to a larger "why" are less prone to emotional fatigue, even during demanding seasons.
- Your calendar should reflect what truly matters. A packed schedule without soul-nourishing tasks is a silent happiness drain.
- Prioritizing self-care, including ample rest and positive self-talk, is essential for sustaining the energy needed to pursue your purpose.

Quick Actionables for Busy Professionals

Category	Actionable	Time Required
Micro-reflection	Ask yourself each morning: "Who do I want to impact today?"	1 min
Weekly reset	Block 15 mins every Sunday to journal: "What gave me energy this week?"	15 mins
Alignment check	Mark one task daily as "purpose-aligned" to remind yourself why it matters	Ongoing
Reignite meaning	Reconnect with an old passion (music, writing, mentoring) for 20 minutes weekly	20 mins/week
Conversation spark	Ask a peer: "What would you love to build, fix, or teach?"	5 mins
Gratitude-as-purpose	End your workday by noting one way you helped someone today	2 mins
Declutter for meaning	Identify one task you can eliminate or delegate—ask: "Does this align with my deeper why?"	10 mins/month
Mindfulness	**Practice presence and mindfulness to fully engage with current sensations and foster emotional well-being.**	5-10 mins/daily
Giving Back	**Look for opportunities to give back to others, as this can activate pleasure centers in the brain and lead to lasting happiness.**	Varied

7.8 Additional Resources

For Busy Professionals Who Want to Go Deeper—Efficiently.

These handpicked resources offer maximum clarity in minimal time. Each is selected for its ability to help professionals uncover, refine, or act on their deeper purpose—without needing to carve out hours from their packed schedules.

Podcasts (Listen while commuting or walking)

- "The Happiness Lab" with Dr. Laurie Santos
    - Episode Recommendation: "The Power of Purpose"

- "WorkLife" by Adam Grant
  - Episode Recommendation: "A Beginner's Guide to Purpose at Work"
- "The Daily Stoic" by Ryan Holiday
  - Short daily reflections on purpose, values, and meaningful work.

Books (For Weekend Reading or Listening)

- "Man's Search for Meaning" – Viktor E. Frankl: A timeless, profound work on finding purpose even in the darkest circumstances.
- "Drive: The Surprising Truth About What Motivates Us" – Daniel H. Pink: Explores autonomy, mastery, and purpose in modern work life.
- "The Power of Meaning" – Emily Esfahani Smith: A practical and philosophical look at purpose through four key pillars.
- "Ikigai: The Japanese Secret to a Long and Happy Life" – Héctor García and Francesc Miralles: For those who want to merge purpose with calm, sustained joy.

Online Tools (Interactive & Action-Oriented)

- Greater Good Science Center – Purpose in Life Quiz
  - Free science-backed test to assess where you stand.
- Ikigai Diagram Generator
  - Visually map your own "reason for being."
- The VIA Character Strengths Survey (Highly recommended)
  - Identify your core values and signature strengths.

Micro-Coaching Apps for Purposeful Living

- Thinkladder (App) – Daily mindset shifts & purpose nudges.
- Intellect (App) – Short mental wellness routines, values & clarity-based.
- Headway (App) – 15-minute book summaries on topics like purpose, values, and vision.

Chapter 8:
Designing Your Environment of Joy & Happiness

8.1 Designing Your Environment for Joy

Why the Environment Shapes How We Feel!

Self-care serves as the cornerstone of general well-being, and designing your environment for joy is a crucial aspect of this holistic approach to happiness.

> "We shape our environment, then our environment shapes us."
> — Winston Churchill

In the relentless pace of modern work life, it's easy to assume that our mood, focus, and well-being are entirely internal matters. But in truth, our external environment silently orchestrates how we feel, think, and behave. The lighting above our heads, the clutter on our desks, the notifications on our phones—they're not just background noise. They are mood sculptors, constantly nudging our nervous systems toward calm or chaos.

The Neuroscience of Environmental Triggers

Studies in environmental psychology and neuroaesthetics show that our brain's emotional processing centers (especially the amygdala and limbic system) are highly sensitive to external stimuli—colors, sounds, smells, textures, and spatial layouts.

- Natural light increases serotonin and stabilizes circadian rhythms.
- Visual clutter elevates cortisol (stress hormone), impairing focus and memory.

- Soothing sounds, greenery, or even nature imagery activate the parasympathetic nervous system (your rest-and-restore mode).
- Smell, processed by the olfactory bulb (directly linked to emotion and memory), can instantaneously shift emotional states—like lavender for calm, or citrus for energy.

This means your environment is never neutral—it's either working for you or against you.

The Emotional Cost of Disorganization

When your workspace is chaotic, your mind mirrors that chaos. Decision fatigue sets in. Attention fragments. Subtle background irritants—like poor lighting, noisy spaces, or clutter piles—act like low-grade stressors, draining your energy without your awareness.

Coaching Insight:

"Your brain is constantly scanning for safety, clarity, and coherence. If your space screams stress, your nervous system listens."

8.2 For Busy Professionals: Why this Matters More than Ever

As someone with back-to-back meetings, deadlines, and responsibilities, you may feel you don't have time to redesign anything. But you're also the one who needs it most.

When your environment is engineered for ease, joy, and focus—even in small pockets—it becomes an ally that restores you instead of depleting you. This intentional design is essential for avoiding burnout and upholding a sustainable, energizing way of life.

- Imagine walking into your workspace and instantly feeling calm.
- Imagine a home entry ritual that releases your work stress in 30 seconds.
- Imagine your phone screen actually grounding you, not triggering comparison or overwhelm.

This isn't about massive makeovers. It's about intentional micro-shifts—small environmental nudges that have big emotional returns.

8.3 Micro-Designing for Joy – At Work and at Home

> "Design is not just what it looks like.
> Design is how it makes you feel."
> — Inspired by Steve Jobs

When you're busy—truly busy—you don't have the luxury of redesigning your entire home or workspace. But here's the truth: you don't need a full renovation to feel renewed. Small, intentional changes can spark profound shifts in how you feel, think, and function.

Let's explore how to reclaim tiny zones of joy in your environment—no matter how tight your schedule.

1. Desk as a Joy Anchor (Not Just a Work Hub)

Your desk isn't just a workstation. It's a psychological cue that tells your brain what mode to be in—overwhelmed and reactive, or focused and composed.

Try This:

- Declutter just 1 square foot of space. Start small and expand weekly.
- Add one emotionally uplifting object: a photo, a quote card, a plant.
- Keep a "Reset Item" nearby: a smooth stone, essential oil roller, or gratitude journal.

Busy Pro Hack: Add a sticky note on your laptop edge:

"What energy am I bringing into this moment?"

2. Mini Green Zones

Research shows that just looking at greenery—even for 40 seconds—can restore concentration and reduce stress. You don't need a backyard; a potted succulent or digital forest screen saver can do the trick.

Ideas for Busy People:

- A desktop plant like snake plant or peace lily (low maintenance, high joy)
- Digital nature: set a calming forest GIF or nature video loop on your second screen
- Rotate a fresh flower every Sunday

3. Soundscapes That Shift Your Mood

Noise is a hidden enemy of emotional balance. Office clatter, traffic, or constant notifications can overload your nervous system. But the right sounds can be medicine.

Quick Wins:

- Use focus music apps (e.g., Noisli, Brain.fm)
- Try sound zoning: headphones with gentle ambient tracks
- Set a "reset ringtone" for your breaks: rain, forest, Tibetan bowls

Coaching Prompt:

"What does peace sound like for you?"

4. Visual Triggers of Calm & Identity

Every visual in your space either adds noise or adds clarity. A quick audit can restore control.

Try This:

- Choose 2–3 images or objects that represent your core values or future vision
- Use a digital vision board as your desktop background
- Replace toxic visual clutter (too many post-its, mixed messages) with one clean mantra or affirmation

Mind-Shift Prompt: "Does my environment reflect who I'm becoming?"

5. Home Transition Rituals: Work to Peace in 60 Seconds

For professionals who work from home, boundaries blur. But happiness lives in transitions.

Create a ritual that tells your nervous system: "Work is done."

- Light a candle at the end of the day
- Change clothes and spritz a calming scent
- Play a specific "unwind" playlist
- Do 10 wall pushups or 1-minute breathwork

You'll be amazed at the psychological reset a ritual provides.

8.4 Digital Spaces – The Emotional Impact of Screens

"Your phone is not just a tool—it's a habitat for your thoughts."

For highly busy professionals, screens are inescapable. Your laptop, your phone, your smartwatch—all connect you to urgent tasks, messages, and decisions. But they also carry a hidden cost: mental clutter, emotional drain, and constant distraction.

Your digital environment is as important as your physical one. It can either be a source of anxiety or a platform for intentional living. Prioritizing your digital health is key to cultivating mental clarity and emotional resilience.

1. Tidy Up Your Phone for Mental Peace

Think of your phone as a personal assistant. Would you want it interrupting you with gossip, chaos, and unnecessary noise?

Minimalist Digital Setup:

- Remove 5 distracting apps from your home screen (yes, even Slack and LinkedIn).
- Move social media into a separate folder labelled "Intentional Time Only."
- Change wallpaper to a calming quote or visual anchor.
- Disable all non-essential notifications.

Micro-Coaching Prompt:

"Does my phone reflect my priorities—or steal them?"

2. Laptop Mindfulness: Create a Calm Desktop

Busy professionals open their laptops at 8 am and often close them well past 8 pm. That's a lot of emotional imprinting on your workspace.

Try These:

- Clear your desktop to show only 5–7 key folders.
- Use a wallpaper that reinforces your mindset ("Calm is a superpower" / "Be here now").
- Turn off all non-urgent pop-ups for 2-hour focus blocks.

Busy Pro Tip:

Install a website blocker like Freedom or Cold Turkey for focused deep work.

3. Email Overload → Emotional Drain

Inbox chaos creates invisible emotional weight. Each unread message is a mental whisper: You're behind.

Quick System for Busy Days:

- Schedule 2 "Email Power Hours" a day (e.g., 11am and 4:30pm).
- Use 3 labels only: Now, Later, Archive.
- If it takes <2 mins, reply now. If not, slot into tomorrow's plan.

Mantra: "I manage email. It doesn't manage me."

4. Tech Timeouts That Don't Break Your Workflow

Digital rest doesn't require long vacations. It requires short, frequent disconnection moments that restore your mental space.

Digital Reset Ideas:

- After every Zoom call: 1-minute eyes-closed breathing reset.
- Between meetings: Walk 10 steps without your phone. Breathe. Look out a window.
- Weekly "Tech Sabbath": 2 hours screen-free on Sunday for reflection or hobbies.

Reminder: Every "unplugged" moment is a gift to your nervous system.

8.5 The Power of Rituals and Tiny Joy Nudges

"Big joy often hides in small, repeated choices."

In a world of constant rush, one of the greatest myths we tell ourselves is: "I don't have time for happiness." But here's the truth—you don't need more time. You need micro-moments that shift energy.

Rituals and joy nudges are like mental vitamins. Small, fast, consistent. They send a message to your brain: "*My well-being matters, even now.*"

Let's explore a toolkit of powerful micro-practices that take less than 2–5 minutes and can change your day.

Morning Anchoring Rituals (1–5 minutes)

Start your day intentionally instead of reactively. Before opening your inbox or social feeds, try one of these:

- Light + Breath: Open your window, take in natural light, and breathe in slowly for 4 counts, out for 6. Reset your nervous system.
- Touchstone Phrase: Whisper a mantra like "I lead with calm" or "One mindful step at a time."
- Micro-journaling: One sentence: "Today, I choose to show up with ___."

Busy Pro Tip: This takes less than your first sip of coffee.

Midday Mindset Nudges

In between back-to-back meetings or tasks, insert tiny joy interrupters to refresh and recenter.

- 2-Minute Movement: Stretch, walk around the block, or do 10 jumping jacks. **Regular physical activity not only improves mood but also boosts energy levels, which are vital for sustained well-being.**
- Aromatherapy Pause: Keep a small roll-on scent (lavender, citrus) at your desk. Inhale with intention.
- Gratitude Reset: Think of one small thing that's going well today—no matter how minor.

Mind Shift Prompt: "What's one thing I'm proud of today—so far?"

Evening Wind-Down Rituals

The way you close the day shapes your emotional recovery.

- Digital Sunset: Set an alarm to turn off screens at least 30 minutes before bed.

- "Let Go" Journaling: Write 3 things you're releasing today (e.g., stress, overthinking, guilt).
- Sleep Cue: Use the same scent, playlist, or lighting every night to trigger rest.

Bonus: Charge your phone outside the bedroom if possible. Your dreams will thank you.

Tiny Joy Nudges Throughout the Day

Even in chaos, insert joy by design:

Nudge Type	Quick Ideas
Visual	Rotate 3 inspiring wallpapers weekly
Audio	Set a "Joy Song" that plays at 2pm daily
Touch	Keep a soft stress ball or grounding stone
Olfactory	Use calming essential oils in the workspace
Kindness	Send one message of appreciation daily

Coaching Reflection

"What if joy wasn't a destination, but a practice?"

Don't wait for the perfect vacation or breakthrough. Start with one ritual. One pause. One smile. When layered over time, these small shifts compound into sustained emotional well-being.

8.6 Action Plan for Busy Professionals

"Clarity beats complexity. Start small, stay consistent."

This section breaks everything down into bite-sized, high-impact moves across four domains: physical space, digital space, rituals, and mindset anchors.

Area	5-Minute Actions	Weekly Boosters	Pro-Level Nudges
Desk/Workspace	Declutter visible surface, light a candle or use a scent diffuser	Refresh a plant, photo or quote near screen	Add soft lighting or calming background music
Digital Habits	Disable 3 non-essential notifications	Create 2x daily email blocks (30 min each)	App detox: Hide 5 apps from home screen
Morning Ritual	Look outside + 3 deep breaths before phone	Pick a 3-word intention for the week	Audio record your intention and replay during commute
Midday Reset	2-minute walk/stretch between meetings	Gratitude Post-It: Write one win each day	Schedule a "joy coffee" with a colleague/friend
Evening Ritual	Phone away 30 min before bed	Journal: 3 things I'm letting go	Use an evening playlist/light to signal wind-down
Mindset Anchors	Choose a weekly affirmation	Use scent or object as physical anchor (e.g., bracelet = "calm")	Set 3 reminders/day with mindset prompts
Sensory Joy	Change wallpaper to calming scene	Keep aromatherapy roll-on at desk	Display a "mood-shifting object" you love

Pro Implementation Tips

- Don't do it all. Start with 1 item per category.
- Stack joy onto existing habits (e.g., gratitude journaling with morning tea).

- Keep it visual: Use sticky notes, phone alarms, or screensavers to nudge you.
- Reflect weekly: What gave you the most lift? Repeat it.

Quick Coaching Prompt:

"If I designed my environment to support joy, what's the one small change I'd make today?"

8.7 Key Learnings + Quick Actionables

Key Learnings for Busy Professionals

SL.no	Insight
1	Your physical and digital environments shape your thoughts and mood more than you realize.
2	Even minor changes (light, scent, clutter, sound) can reduce stress and boost positivity.
3	Rituals anchor your mindset; they don't need to be long, but they must be consistent.
4	Joy can be intentionally designed into your day—using visual cues, micro-habits, and sensory triggers.
5	You don't need more time—just better alignment between space, habits, and happiness.

Quick Actionables for the Time-Starved Professional

Daily Actions (under 5 mins)

- Look outside and take 3 deep breaths before phone.
- Clear one item from your workspace each day.
- Disable 3 notifications that distract you.
- Whisper a morning mantra while brushing teeth.
- End day by asking: "What felt good today?"

Weekly Actions (under 15 mins)

- Refresh your desk with a photo, quote, or object that sparks joy.
- Build a "mood reset" playlist for commute or lunch breaks.
- Block 30 minutes for a personal recharge activity (walk, call, hobby). **Remember, making time for enjoyable activities is a powerful emotional reset that promotes fulfillment and optimism.**
- Write down 1 thing that lifted your mood—and repeat it next week.

Monthly Reset (30–45 mins)

- Declutter a key area (desktop, inbox, shelf) that feels overwhelming.
- Redesign one space—your bedside, your home desk, or your Zoom background—for inspiration.
- Reflect: "What small tweak this month made me feel most alive?"

Remember: consistency, not complexity, is the key to sustainable joy.

8.8 Additional Resources

For Busy Professionals — Practical Links to Reinforce Daily Joy

Podcasts for a Joy-Designed Life

(Episodes mostly 10–20 mins — ideal for commute, coffee, or wind-down)

- The Happiness Lab with Dr. Laurie Santos
  - Science-backed episodes from Yale professor exploring everyday joy.
- Daily Calm – from Calm App
  - Daily 10-minute meditations to start or reset your day with peace.
- Optimal Living Daily
  - Summarized wisdom from top blogs on minimalism, habits, and happiness.

Books That Deliver Big Value in Little Time

- *Atomic Habits* – by James Clear: Transform your surroundings to support better habits. https://jamesclear.com/atomic-habits
- *Joyful* – by Ingrid Fetell Lee: How colors, shapes, and surroundings boost happiness. https://aestheticsofjoy.com/joyful-book
- *The Power of Moments* – by Chip & Dan Heath: How small experiences and rituals create lasting impact. https://heathbrothers.com/the-power-of-moments

TED Talks – High Inspiration in Short Bursts

- Where Joy Hides—and How to Find It – Ingrid Fetell Lee
  - A powerful talk on designing joy through everyday surroundings.
- The Surprising Science of Happiness – Dan Gilbert
  - Harvard psychologist on how we generate happiness internally.

Apps That Make Joy a Habit

App	Purpose	Link
Fabulous	Morning rituals and habit coaching	https://www.thefabulous.co
Forest	Stay focused by planting virtual trees	https://www.forestapp.cc
Calm	Sleep, mindfulness & mental reset	https://www.calm.com
Insight Timer	Thousands of guided meditations	https://insighttimer.com
Brilliant Quotes Widget	Daily quote widget for lock/home screen	https://play.google.com/store/apps/details?id=com.ishant.bq

One Last Coaching Prompt for You

"If your workspace or schedule could whisper one word to lift your mood… what would it say?"

Chapter 9:
Time, Priorities & Myths of Work – Life Balance

9.1 Time, Priorities & the Myth of Balance

How to Redesign Time Around What Truly Matters, especially for busy professionals who feel stretched, time-poor, and constantly juggling competing demands.

This chapter isn't just about managing your calendar; it's about a fundamental shift in how you relate to your time, prioritizing what truly energizes and fulfills you. It's about moving from simply **"doing more"** to **"doing what matters"** and embracing a more intentional way of living.

9.2 The Great Myth of Work-Life Balance

We have all heard it: "You need better work-life balance."

It sounds sensible—like a noble pursuit. But here's the truth:

Work-life balance is a myth—especially for busy professionals.

Balance implies an even scale, a perfect 50/50 division between "work" and "life." But life isn't a spreadsheet. Your energy shifts. Your focus pivots. Some days work demands more; other days, family or health do. And that's okay. Life is more like a dynamic equalizer, where different frequencies ebb and flow. The goal isn't static perfection, but a responsive, flexible approach that honors your current needs and long-term vision.

Trying to "balance" everything equally creates guilt, anxiety, and unrealistic expectations. You feel like you're always failing something.

Instead, what you truly need is:

Alignment. Intention. Rhythm.

What if the real goal isn't to balance your life perfectly...
...but to design your time around what brings meaning, energy, and joy?

9.3 Time, Energy, and Attention — The Real Resources

Time is not your most limited resource.

It's the alignment of your time, energy, and attention that matters. Understanding your personal rhythms and what truly fuels (or drains) you is the first step in mastering these currencies.

Time

You have 24 hours. Everyone does. But how you spend them makes all the difference. Are you constantly reacting to others' demands—or proactively investing in what matters?

Energy

Different tasks require different kinds of energy—creative, emotional, physical. And your energy fluctuates. Protecting your peak energy hours is more powerful than squeezing more into your calendar.

Attention

Where your focus goes, your life flows. But in a distracted, hyper-connected world, attention is fragmented. The key is to intentionally place your attention where it creates the most joy or results.

Coaching Reflection:

"What drains you the most—time scarcity, energy depletion, or distracted attention?"

9.4 The Happiness Blocks Method – Reclaiming Joy in Your Calendar

If you're like most busy professionals, your calendar is packed before the week even starts—meetings, deadlines, family responsibilities, and digital clutter. There's barely space to breathe, let alone plan joy.

But here's the key insight:

If you don't block time for happiness, the world will schedule over it.

What Are Happiness Blocks?

Happiness Blocks are intentional, non-negotiable, calendar-guarded time slots that reconnect you to what truly matters.

They're not bonus moments you squeeze in when "everything else is done."

They're the first things you protect—because they fuel everything else. Think of them not as breaks, but as strategic investments in your long-term resilience and sustained performance. Consistent, even small, blocks compound over time into profound well-being.

Types of Happiness Blocks for Busy Lives

Block Type	Duration	Examples	Why It Matters
Micro Joy Breaks	5–10 mins	Nature walk, music pause, mindful tea sip	Restores clarity and joy in-between intense work sprints
Core Connection Time	20–30 mins	Lunch with loved one, call with friend, storytime w/ kids	Nurtures relationships that nourish you
Flow & Focus Power Hour	60 mins	Deep work, creative thinking, strategy session	Aligns with peak energy for meaningful work
Recharge Rituals	10–15 mins	Afternoon meditation, nap, journaling	Boosts mental energy and reduces burnout risk
Mini-Learning Block	20–30 mins	Read a book, listen to a podcast, attend a webinar	Keeps your mind fresh and future-ready

How to Start Using Happiness Blocks (Even If You're Crazy Busy)

1. **Audit Your Calendar**
    - Highlight time spent on autopilot vs. what fuels you
    - Identify one 15-minute slot daily to begin
2. **Name the Block**
    - Don't label it "free time." Use purpose-driven labels:
        - "Soul Recharge," "Relationship Refuel," "Gratitude Reset"
3. **Protect It Like a Meeting**
    - Set reminders. Turn off notifications. Be present.
    - Let your assistant/team/family know this is non-negotiable time.
4. **Start Small but Be Consistent**
    - 10 minutes daily is better than 1 hour once a month.

5. **Track the Ripple Effect**
    - Keep a short log: How did this block affect your day? Your mood?
    - You'll likely find productivity increases, not decreases.

Coaching Prompt:

"If joy had a space on your calendar, when would it be—and what would you do?"

9.5 Mindful Scheduling – The Art of Saying 'No' with Grace

If you feel like your schedule owns you (instead of the other way around), you're not alone.

"Every time you say yes to something unaligned, you're saying no to something meaningful."

Busyness often comes not from bad time management, but from boundary collapse. When every meeting invite gets a "yes," every errand feels urgent, and every digital ping gets your attention, your priorities vanish under a pile of obligations.

Why Saying 'No' is a Happiness Habit

Saying 'no' is not about shutting people down. It's about saying 'yes' to your deeper values. Saying 'no' isn't a refusal; it's an act of clear communication and self-stewardship that creates the necessary space for your highest priorities.

Busy professionals often:

- Say yes to protect relationships
- Avoid conflict or guilt
- Fear missing opportunities

But here's the truth:

The happiest, highest-performing professionals are excellent at saying no calmly, early, and kindly.

Coaching Reframes for Saying No

Instead of defaulting to "I will try" or "Maybe," try these aligned, respectful responses:

Situation	Instead of This...	Try Saying This
Non-essential meeting	"Sure, I will join."	"Thanks for including me. I will stay looped via notes."
Social obligation	"Okay, I will come."	"I'd love to catch up soon, but I'm keeping this evening quiet."
New project ask	"Let me take it on."	"This is valuable—can we revisit next quarter when I have more bandwidth?"
Family/friend ask	"I will do it all."	"I want to support you. Can we find a time that works better for both of us?"

3-Minute Micro Tool: The Boundary Buffer

1. **Pause** before replying to a new ask.
2. **Ask yourself:** Does this align with my top 3 values or goals right now?
3. If no, respond with kindness but clarity.
4. Suggest alternatives if helpful (delegate, delay, digital follow-up).

This tiny pause can save hours of misaligned action—and restore your energy.

Mini Reflection Prompt:

"What's one thing I need to start saying no to, so I can say yes to what matters?"

9.6 Templates and Examples – How High Performers Protect Their Time

Beyond theory, the true power of time mastery lies in its practical application. Here's how leading professionals operationalize these principles to create truly impactful and joyful schedules.

Busy professionals often believe that being constantly available is the price of success. But in reality:

The most effective leaders protect their time like they protect their energy.

They don't chase productivity—they engineer it.

Let's decode how.

1. The "Ideal Week" Template

Used by: High-performance coaches, executives, solo entrepreneurs

This simple structure helps align time with values—not just tasks.

Day	Morning (8–11am)	Midday (11am–2pm)	Afternoon (2–5pm)	Evening
Monday	Focused Deep Work	Admin + Emails	1-on-1s or Meetings	Family Time
Tuesday	Strategy Block	Lunch + Recharge	Client Delivery	Gym/Walk
Wednesday	Creative Thinking	Team Sync	No Meetings (Flow Time)	Reading
Thursday	Teaching/Training	Community Engagement	Feedback/Reviews	Quiet Time
Friday	Weekly Review + Goals	Light Work + Wrap-up	Early Shut Down	Social/Rest

Start by blocking what matters most—relationships, learning, creativity. Then fit in the rest.

2. Time Blocking + Theme Days

Used by: Elon Musk, Cal Newport, Deep Work advocates, including myself

Break your week into theme blocks (e.g., Monday = Strategic Thinking, Wednesday = Creation Day) and protect 90–120 min blocks for deep work.

Example:

"10–11:30am Tuesday = Strategy Deep Work (Phone Off, No Email)"

3. The "Daily 3 Wins" Journal

Used by: Busy professionals who resist over-scheduling

At the start of each day:

- Write down 3 wins you want to feel proud of by evening.
- Include 1 personal moment of joy, not just work.

Example:

1. Finish proposal draft
2. Eat lunch without distractions
3. 10-min walk with my daughter

Why it works: Focus on impact, not volume. Builds a bias toward intentional effort.

4. Email Boundary Script (Copy-Paste Friendly)

Instead of being reactive to every email…

Auto-responder or signature line:

"Thanks for your message. I check email twice daily (10am and 4pm) to stay focused on high-priority work. I will respond as soon as possible."

→ Trains others to respect your time rhythms.

Example 1: Manuella, VP in a Tech Firm

Challenge: Constant back-to-back Zoom calls, burnout, poor sleep.

Fix:

- Introduced 30-min joy block at 7am (walk + tea with no phone)
- Batched internal meetings to Tue/Thu only
- Set Slack hours to 10am–5pm only

Result: Felt calmer, clearer-headed, and actually looked forward to mornings again.

Example 2: Raj, Senior Consultant at a Global Firm

Challenge:

Raj was always "on." He worked 10–12 hours daily across time zones, checked emails late into the night, and missed out on quality time with family.

Shift Implemented:

- Introduced a hard stop at 7:00 PM each weekday with a visible calendar block titled: "Family Hour – Non-Negotiable."
- Shifted morning email check to after 20-minute breathing + intention ritual.
- Created a "deep work sprint" block daily from 9:30–11:00 AM, during which notifications were muted.

Results:

Raj said: "I don't feel behind anymore. Ironically, I'm more productive with fewer hours. And my kids feel like I'm mentally present—not just physically home."

Example 3: Anika, Entrepreneur & Wellness Coach

Challenge:

Anika was passionate about her work but overwhelmed by content creation, client sessions, and managing her brand solo. Her energy was burned out by multitasking.

Shift Implemented:

- Adopted Theme Days:
    - Mon/Wed = Client Coaching
    - Tue = Content Creation
    - Thu = Business Admin
    - Fri = Learning & Nature Walks
- Created a "No-Scroll Zone" from 9 AM–12 PM: no social media, no distractions.
- Added a 15-minute Joy Ritual post-lunch: playlist + tea + balcony time.

Results:

"My creative energy has come back. I feel in charge of my time, instead of feeling like I was being pulled in 10 directions."

9.7 Key Learnings + Quick Actionables

Designed for High Performers & Time-Starved Professionals

Key Learnings

1. Work-life balance is a myth.

   Strive for alignment, not perfection. Happiness grows when your time reflects your values—not when you try to split everything 50/50.

2. Time, energy, and attention are your true currencies.

   Guard them. Schedule your highest-focus work for your peak energy hours. Redirect attention to what matters—intentionally.

3. The calendar is your mirror.

   If joy, recovery, or meaningful connection isn't in your calendar, it probably isn't happening. Don't just schedule meetings—schedule happiness blocks.

4. Tiny rituals matter more than big resolutions.

   A 3-minute mindset priming or a 15-minute walk can shift your mental state more effectively than a 2-week vacation you can't take.

5. High performers aren't available all the time.

   They are protectively invisible during their focus zones. Boundaries are not about avoidance—they're tools for intentional living.

Quick Actionables for Busy Professionals

Action	Time Needed	Impact Area
Block 15 mins daily as a "Happiness Block" for joy, movement, or silence	15 min/day	Mental Reset + Emotional Recharge
Set calendar themes (e.g., Mon = Strategy, Wed = Creation)	30 min/week planning	Focus + Flow
Use "3 Wins Journal" each morning	5 min/day	Clarity + Positivity
Set email/Slack boundaries and communicate them	1-time setup	Energy + Distraction Control
Protect 90-min Deep Work block during peak hours	90 min/day	Productivity + Satisfaction
Do a Sunday 10-min Weekly Intentional Planning	10 min/week	Strategic Focus
Batch meetings into 2 specific days	Ongoing	Calendar Control + Reduced Switching
Try 1 Ritualized Joy Nudge (e.g., evening walk, playlist)	10–15 min/day	Dopamine Boost + Presence

Coaching Reflection:

"If your time was your team—would you fire how it's currently managed?"

"What one shift this week would move you 1% closer to a joyful rhythm?"

9.8 Additional Resources for Time & Priority Mastery

Whether you have 2 minutes or 20, these trusted resources will help you take powerful steps toward time alignment, energy renewal, and happiness-centered productivity.

Books (Short Reads or Listen-Alongs)

Title	Author	Format	Why It's Useful
Essentialism: The Disciplined Pursuit of Less	Greg McKeown	Audiobook / Kindle	Helps simplify decisions and protect your time with clarity
The One Thing	Gary Keller	Audiobook / Kindle	A framework to focus on what truly matters, daily
Make Time	Jake Knapp & John Zeratsky	Paperback / eBook	80+ smart hacks to reclaim control of your day
Deep Work	Cal Newport	Audiobook / Paperback	Techniques to master focused time in a distracted world

Podcasts (Great While Walking or Commuting)

Podcast	Host	Recommended Episode
The Tim Ferriss Show	Tim Ferriss	"Time Management Lessons from Top Performers"
The Daily Stoic	Ryan Holiday	3–5 min mindset resets on clarity and time
The Productivity Show	Asian Efficiency	"5 Rituals that Save You 10+ Hours Weekly"

Free Tools & Planners

Tool	Link	What It Does
Sunsama	sunsama.com	Daily planner that aligns tasks with calendar & values
Clockwise	getclockwise.com	Automates meeting scheduling to protect focus blocks
Notion – Weekly Intentional Planner Template	notion.so	Download pre-built templates for energy-aware planning
Toggl Track	toggl.com	Helps identify time drains and optimize for deep work
The Eisenhower Matrix	eisenhower.me	Prioritization tool for urgent vs. important tasks

2-Minute Daily Practices

- **Morning Mindset Ritual:** Ask "What matters most today?" before emails.
- **"One Tab Rule":** Only keep one browser tab open during deep work.
- **8–8 Digital Fast:** No emails or social after 8 PM. Start fresh at 8 AM.

Final Tip for Busy Readers:

"You don't need more time—you need fewer distractions, better energy alignment, and a life that reflects what you care about most."

When your time reflects your values, happiness isn't a distant ideal—it's built into the rhythm of your days.

Chapter 10:

Sustainable Self – Care for Busy Professionals

Because You Can't Pour from an Empty Cup!

10.1 Redefining Self-Care Beyond Spa Days

For many professionals, the term "self-care" feels indulgent—like bubble baths, green smoothies, or a Sunday yoga class that gets canceled every other week.

But real, sustainable self-care? It's none of that fluff—and all of what truly helps you function and flourish.

Self-care isn't a luxury. It's your infrastructure.

Especially when you're a high-performer running on depleted energy and maxed-out responsibilities.

True self-care is about taking care of your:

- **Emotions** before they boil over
- **Mind** before it frays
- **Body** before it breaks down
- **Spirit** before it disconnects from meaning

And for busy professionals, it must be time-aware, guilt-free, and systemized—not added as another overwhelming item on a to-do list.

Quick Self-Care Diagnostic: Where Are You Running on Empty?

Rate yourself honestly. Awareness is the first step toward sustainable change.

Instructions:

For each area, rate your agreement with the statements on a scale from 1 to 5 (1 = Strongly Disagree, 5 = Strongly Agree)

Mental Well-being

Statement	Rating (1–5)
I can focus without constant distraction or mental fog.	
I get regular breaks from screen time and mental overload.	
I feel mentally sharp and creative most days.	

Emotional Health

Statement	Rating (1–5)
I feel emotionally supported by people around me.	
I am able to express emotions instead of suppressing them.	
I feel calm or emotionally balanced even during tough days.	

Physical Energy

Statement	Rating (1–5)
I sleep enough to feel rested most mornings.	
I move my body at least 3–4 times a week.	
I eat to nourish—not just to survive.	

Spiritual Alignment (Purpose & Values)

Statement	Rating (1–5)
I feel a sense of meaning in how I spend my time.	
I feel connected to something bigger—purpose, values, or impact.	
I regularly pause to reflect, reset, or reconnect.	

Scoring Guide

- **36–45:** You're thriving. Keep reinforcing what's working.
- **26–35:** You're stable, but a few areas need tune-up.
- **16–25:** Caution zone. Start building better boundaries and recovery time.

- **Below 15:** Burnout risk. It's time to prioritize your well-being proactively.

10.2 Emotional, Mental, Physical & Spiritual Renewal

Simple, sustainable shifts that refuel your inner battery—even when time is scarce.

1. Emotional Renewal: Regulate, Don't Suppress

Busy professionals often suppress emotions to stay "professional." But over time, unprocessed emotions leak into irritability, exhaustion, or disengagement.

Mini Rituals for Emotional Health (under 5 minutes):

- **The 90-Second Reset Rule:** Pause, name the emotion ("I feel anxious"), breathe through it for 90 seconds. This interrupts spirals.
- **Emotional Debrief Prompt (daily):** "What's the emotion I avoided today? What did it need from me?"
- **2-Minute Vent Walks:** Walk and talk (to yourself, a voice memo, or a trusted friend). Label → release → reset.

Coaching Insight: Emotions aren't interruptions—they're data. Listen early before they shout later.

2. Mental Renewal: Declutter Your Brain

The always-on culture leads to mental overload, which silently erodes your clarity, memory, and decision-making.

Quick Practices for Mental Clarity:

- **Brain Dump Journal (3 mins before bed):** Write down everything on your mind—no order, no judgment. Clears cognitive clutter.
- **The "One-Tab Rule":** Only one browser tab for deep work. Multitasking is the enemy of mental clarity.
- **10-Minute Focus Sprint:** Use tools like pomofocus.io to train your brain back into focus through time-blocked sprints.

Coaching Insight: Your brain isn't designed to hold everything—it's designed to process one thing well at a time.

3. Physical Renewal: Nourish, Move, Rest

You don't need a 90-minute gym session to recharge physically. The right micro-habits can be transformative.

Small Physical Wins That Stack Up:

- **Movement Snacks:** 5 squats or 10 wall push-ups every 90 minutes of sitting.
- **Hydration Prompt:** Set 3 alarms labeled "Recharge, don't deplete" to drink water.
- **The 3-2-1 Sleep Method:** No food 3 hours before bed, no work 2 hours before, no screens 1 hour before.

Research shows: Just 20 minutes of movement boosts endorphins and sharpens focus for hours.

4. Spiritual Renewal: Reconnect to Purpose & Meaning

You don't need to meditate on a mountaintop to feel spiritually aligned. Just moments of intentional reconnection.

Quick Anchors to Realign with Your Deeper Self:

- **"Why" Whisper Prompt:** Ask yourself once a day, "Why does what I'm doing matter?"
- **Mini Gratitude Ritual:** In your shower, list 3 things you're grateful for—no phone needed, no extra time.
- **Quiet Commute Time:** No podcast, no email. Just silence. Let your thoughts settle. Let your being catch up with your doing.

Coaching Insight: When your day starts to feel transactional, it's time to pause for perspective.

Quick Renewal Strategies for Busy Professionals

Renewal Domain	Practice/Tool	Time Required	Benefit
Emotional	90-Second Reset Rule	90 seconds	Interrupts emotional spirals
Emotional	Emotional Debrief Prompt	2 mins	Increases emotional awareness
Emotional	2-Minute Vent Walks	2 mins	Releases stress real-time
Mental	Brain Dump Journal	3 mins	Declutters mind before sleep
Mental	One-Tab Rule	Ongoing	Boosts deep work focus
Mental	10-Minute Focus Sprint	10 mins	Sharpens mental clarity
Physical	Movement Snacks	1-2 mins	Boosts energy & posture
Physical	Hydration Prompt	3x/day	Supports hydration & energy
Physical	3-2-1 Sleep Method	Evening routine	Improves sleep quality
Spiritual	Why Whisper Prompt	1 min	Reconnects to purpose
Spiritual	Mini Gratitude Ritual	2 mins	Builds positive emotion baseline
Spiritual	Quiet Commute Time	During commute	Facilitates reflection & calm

10.3 Self-Care Traps to Avoid

Even with the best intentions, busy professionals often misunderstand or misapply self-care. This section reveals the most common traps—and how to avoid them—so that your efforts genuinely replenish rather than exhaust you.

Trap 1: Treating Self-Care as a "To-Do" List

Many professionals reduce self-care to checkboxes—spa, workout, meal prep. While structure is helpful, when these become obligations rather than rejuvenations, the joy is lost.

Reframe: Ask yourself, "Does this give me energy or just fill my calendar?"

Coaching Prompt: Are you performing self-care… or actually feeling cared for?

Trap 2: Confusing Escape with Restoration

Netflix binges, shopping sprees, doom-scrolling—these may feel good in the moment but rarely leave us feeling renewed. They provide numbing, not nourishment.

Reframe: Choose activities that replenish energy, not just distract you from depletion.

Coaching Prompt: After this activity, do I feel more grounded or more drained?

Trap 3: Over Personalizing Burnout

Professionals often blame themselves for not coping well—"Maybe I'm not resilient enough." But burnout is often systemic, not personal.

Reframe: Instead of internalizing stress, assess environmental causes—unreasonable demands, lack of boundaries, or unclear expectations.

Coaching Prompt: What part of my burnout is about me—and what part is about the system I'm in?

Trap 4: Believing You Need "More Time" for Self-Care

One of the most dangerous myths. You don't need more time—you need tiny but consistent interventions.

Reframe: Start with micro-practices that take 1–5 minutes. Done daily, they add up.

Coaching Prompt: What can I do in the next 2 minutes to feel 2% better?

Trap 5: Self-Care Without Boundaries

It's impossible to refill your cup if it has a leak. If you're constantly people-pleasing or afraid to say "No," your energy will always drain—no matter how many bubble baths or journaling sessions you schedule.

Reframe: The most powerful self-care is saying "No" to what doesn't serve you.

Coaching Prompt: Where do I need to set a loving, clear boundary this week?

Trap 6: Waiting for Burnout to Hit Before Acting

Too many people wait until they're exhausted, irritable, or physically unwell before investing in care.

Reframe: Make self-care proactive, not reactive. Like brushing your teeth, it's maintenance—not crisis management.

Coaching Prompt: What would my week look like if I prioritized energy first, not last?

10.4 Personal Self-Care Planning Guide

A 5-Step Framework for Designing a Self-Care System That Fits Into Your Real Life

Why You Need a Self-Care System, Not Just Moments

Busy professionals don't need one-off spa days. They need repeatable, low-effort, high-impact rituals that create real change in energy, mindset, and resilience.

This guide helps you build that—your own self-care ecosystem—on your terms.

Step 1: Identify Your Top 3 Energy Zones

Reflect on where you need the most renewal right now.

Energy Zone	Ask Yourself...
Mental Energy	Am I constantly overthinking, distracted, or unable to focus?
Emotional Energy	Am I feeling heavy, irritable, or emotionally drained?
Physical Energy	Am I tired, sluggish, or getting frequent body aches?
Spiritual Energy	Am I feeling disconnected from meaning or purpose?

Action: Write down your Top 2 Zones that feel most depleted. These are your self-care priorities.

Step 2: Choose 1–2 Micro-Practices for Each Zone

Don't aim for perfection. Focus on easy-to-implement habits that work for you. Here are examples:

Zone	Micro-Practice (2–10 mins)
Mental	Morning journaling, Pomodoro break, phone-free lunch
Emotional	Breathwork pause, music therapy, talk to a trusted friend
Physical	10-min stretch, hydration habit, posture reset
Spiritual	Gratitude journaling, nature walk, values check-in

Action: Choose 1 micro-practice per priority zone. Anchor them to existing routines (e.g., after brushing teeth).

Step 3: Create Your Weekly Ritual Grid

Design simple rituals around your natural rhythms.

Day	Morning Ritual	Midday Reset	Evening Recharge
Monday	2-min deep breathing	Walk after lunch	Gratitude reflection
Tuesday	Positive intention	Music & movement	Digital detox window
...	...	...	...

Pro Tip: Focus on consistency over intensity. A 3-minute reset every day beats a 1-hour retreat once a month.

Step 4: Add Accountability & Reflection

You're more likely to stick with something you track or share.

- Use a habit tracker or journal
- Share your 1-minute ritual with a friend or colleague
- Use reminder apps (e.g., Loop Habit Tracker, Done)

Reflection Prompt (Weekly):

"What tiny self-care moment brought me the most peace this week?"

Step 5: Set a Self-Care Theme for the Month

One clear theme per month helps maintain intentionality.

Examples:

- **March:** "Calm Over Chaos"
- **April:** "Strengthen My Sleep"
- **May:** "Move More, Stress Less"

Action: Write your monthly theme at the top of your planner or mirror.

10.5 Rituals for Even Your Busiest Days

"Small hinges swing big doors."

These are micro-habits—low-effort, high-impact rituals you can weave into your daily flow. They require no drastic lifestyle change, just small, intentional tweaks.

Morning Launch Rituals (Time: 2–5 min)

Your morning state sets the tone for your mental resilience and emotional availability.

Ritual	What to Do	Why It Works
Breathe Before Screens	3 deep breaths before checking your phone	Shifts you from reactivity to intentionality
One-Word Intent	Ask: "What energy do I want to carry today?"	Primes your mindset to align with values
Sunlight First	Open window or step outside for 60 sec	Boosts alertness and mood (vitamin D + circadian reset)

Midday Mindset Resets (Time: 1–3 min)

Interrupt autopilot mode. Reclaim clarity.

Ritual	What to Do	Why It Works
Desk Stand + Stretch	3 shoulder rolls + 5 deep breaths	Reduces cortisol; prevents stiffness & mental fatigue
Power Pause	Put your hand on your chest and ask: "What story am I telling myself?"	Creates emotional awareness & control
Hydration Reboot	Drink 1 full glass of water mindfully	Improves focus, energy, and decision-making

Evening Wind-Down Anchors (Time: 5–10 min)

These rituals signal your body and mind: "You are safe to rest."

Ritual	What to Do	Why It Works
Digital Dimmer	Switch off screens 30 mins before sleep	Melatonin boost; better sleep quality
Gratitude Gaze	Write 3 micro-moments you appreciated today	Trains optimism and reduces mental clutter
Foot-on-Floor Pause	Sit on your bed, feet grounded, 3 deep breaths	Anchors nervous system before sleep

Weekly Anchoring Rituals (Time: 10–15 min once a week)

A simple system to course-correct and build intentional joy.

Ritual	What to Do	Why It Works
Sunday Self-Scan	Ask: "What fueled me? What drained me? What do I need more/less of?"	Aligns your week with your values, not autopilot
Happiness Block Planning	Add 3 non-negotiable joy moments to your calendar	Ensures joy becomes a scheduled priority

Coaching Insight:

"Don't wait for a vacation to feel well. Build your wellness into your week."

10.6 Key Learnings + Quick Actionables

"What you repeat becomes who you are."

Key Learnings

- Self-care is not indulgent—it's intelligent.

  Burnout is more expensive than prevention. Strategic self-care is a performance enhancer, not a luxury.

- True renewal is multi-dimensional.

  Happiness and resilience rise when you integrate emotional, mental, physical, and spiritual micro-recoveries.

- Rituals > Routines.

  Small, intentional acts—even 3-minute check-ins—have compounding effects on joy, clarity, and energy.

- Awareness precedes transformation.
- Most professionals don't lack time—they lack clarity on where their energy is leaking and where renewal is possible.
- You don't rise to the level of your goals; you fall to the level of your systems.

  The right self-care rituals turn self-neglect into self-leadership.

Quick Actionables for Busy Professionals

Timing	Action	Purpose
Today	Choose 1 micro-ritual from each category (morning, midday, evening) and schedule it	Start building your "wellness scaffolding"
This Week	Do a 10-min Self-Care Audit using the diagnostic quiz (from Section 1)	Spot your biggest gaps—and most immediate fixes
Every Morning	Name your 1-word emotional intent for the day	Begin the day on purpose, not autopilot
Every Friday	Ask: "What part of my energy was ignored this week?"	Course correct before burnout compounds
Next 7 Days	Plan 3 Happiness Blocks in your calendar (see Chapter 8)	Protect joyful moments like meetings—because they matter

10.7 Additional Resources

These carefully selected resources offer concise, science-backed, and actionable insights. Each one has been chosen to serve professionals with limited time—but a deep desire to sustain their energy, clarity, and emotional resilience.

Listen – Short & Powerful Podcasts

Title	Format	Link	Why It Helps
The Happiness Lab with Dr. Laurie Santos	Podcast	https://www.happinesslab.fm	Yale professor explores practical happiness science—one episode at a time
On Being with Krista Tippett	Podcast	https://onbeing.org/series/podcast/	Deep, reflective conversations on life, meaning, rest, and soul
Ten Percent Happier with Dan Harris	Podcast	https://www.tenpercent.com/podcast	Micro-interviews on mindfulness and emotional strength for high performers

Read – Short Reads & Guides

Title	Format	Link	Why It Helps
Self-Care Isn't Just Indulgence – HBR	Article	https://hbr.org/2021/03/self-care-isnt-just-indulgence	Reframes self-care as an executive-level responsibility
Greater Good Magazine – UC Berkeley	Articles & Tools	https://greatergood.berkeley.edu	Offers gratitude practices, stress reduction tools, and emotional literacy research
Mindful.org	Article Portal	https://www.mindful.org	Offers daily mindfulness tips, workplace well-being articles, and reflection tools

Use – Free Planners & Toolkits

Title	Format	Link	Why It Helps
Self-Care Starter Kit – University at Buffalo	Toolkit	https://socialwork.buffalo.edu/resources/self-care-starter-kit.html	Includes burnout checklists, energy renewal ideas, and habit tracking
Mental Health America: Workplace Wellness	Toolkit & Exercises	https://mhanational.org/workplace-wellness	Customizable for professionals, includes stress audits and recovery plans
Self-Care Assessment Worksheet – Therapist Aid	Worksheet (PDF)	https://www.therapistaid.com/worksheets/self-care-assessment.pdf	Practical tool to help map and maintain physical, emotional, and relational care

Busy Reader Tip:

Bookmark just one resource per category this week. Create a "Self-Care HQ" folder in your browser for quick access during breaks or weekends.

Chapter 11:
The Happiness Compass

11.1 Why You Need a Personal Compass—Especially When Time is Scarce

Busy professionals often operate at full throttle. Goals are chased, calendars are packed, and life moves fast. But speed without direction only leads to burnout or emptiness. That's why this chapter invites you to pause—not to stop—but to realign.

"A compass doesn't move you forward. It keeps you aligned with your true direction."

Your Happiness Compass is that inner framework. It's the integration of everything you've learned—clarity about your values, your rituals, your energy, and the meaning you assign to success.

It answers a fundamental question:

What would your ideal life feel like, even on a busy Monday morning?

11.2 Recap – The Core Tools, Habits, and Mindsets You've Collected

Here's a consolidated view of what your toolkit now includes:

Theme	Key Tools & Habits	Purpose
Mindset	Reframing, Journaling, Morning Priming, Reset Breaks	Reset thoughts and emotions fast
Habits	Movement, Sleep, Nutrition, Hobbies, "Doing Nothing"	Fuel body-mind resilience
Emotions	Emotional labeling, self-compassion, gratitude	Navigate stress with clarity
Relationships	Micro-connections, boundary rituals, appreciation	Multiply happiness through connection
Purpose	Life Timeline, Ikigai, Weekly Meaning Check-ins	Align actions with deep meaning
Time Design	Happiness Blocks, Time-Energy-Attention framework	Optimize limited time for joy
Self-Care	10-min rituals, digital detoxes, renewal systems	Sustain energy and performance

11.3 Build Your Personal Happiness Framework

A Happiness Compass has 4 points:

North: Purpose

- Why do I do what I do?
- What deeper impact fuels me—even on hard days?

East: Daily Practices

- What are the non-negotiable habits that keep me grounded?
- These are 10-minute wins that protect my energy.

South: Relationships

- Who nourishes me? Who drains me?

- How can I connect meaningfully, even in short bursts?

West: Mindset & Recovery

- What stories am I believing? Are they helping me grow?
- What are my quick recovery tools after stress or failure?

Coaching Reflection Prompt:

"Am I living by design—or by default?"

11.4 Crafting Your Action Plan (Minimalist but Powerful)

Step	Prompt	Example
1	Identify one feeling you want more of each day	"I want to feel calm in the chaos."
2	Define 3 micro-habits to generate that feeling	1) Deep breath before meetings, 2) Walk post-lunch, 3) Gratitude text daily
3	Schedule one weekly check-in	Sunday 10 mins: Reflect, realign, reset
4	Remove one thing that blocks happiness	"No screens post 10pm" or "Say no to non-essential meetings"

Busy Professional Hack: Save these 4 steps as a weekly email to yourself titled "My Compass Reset."

11.5 Final Coaching Reflection – Let This Be Your New Normal

You don't need to overhaul your life.

You need to align your existing life—your work, routines, relationships—with what truly matters to you.

"The happiest professionals aren't those with more time. They're the ones who use small time pockets wisely—to reconnect, reframe, and realign."

Your **Happiness Compass** is not another to-do list. It's your living, breathing guide. It reminds you who you are, what you care about, and how to live fully—even on the busiest days.

Your Journey Forward – The Happiness Within Reach

Dear Reader,

As you reach the final chapter of this book, take a moment to pause and acknowledge yourself.

In a world that demands so much of you—your time, your energy, your expertise—you chose to invest a few sacred hours in something rare: your own happiness. That alone makes you a visionary.

This book has not just been about happiness—it's been about you.

Your unique rhythms.

Your hidden aspirations.

Your silent battles.

Your longing for more peace, meaning, and joy amid the deadlines and dashboards.

You've walked through chapters on mindset, habits, purpose, relationships, time, and self-care—not as abstract theories, but as lived tools crafted for high performers like you. You now carry with you a compass: not to someone else's version of success, but to your own version of a life well lived.

What We have Discovered Together:

- **Happiness is not a luxury; it's a daily choice**—and a powerful form of productivity.
- Your **mindset**, not your metrics, determines how much joy you extract from life.
- **Relationships**, not resumes, are the strongest predictors of well-being.
- **Purpose** turns even the busiest schedules into deeply meaningful lives.
- Your **environment**, rituals, and time choices shape how your inner world feels.

What Comes Next?

- Keep the Tools Alive

  Use the quick actionables, worksheets, and nudges as anchors in your week. Don't wait for overwhelm to arrive—proactively protect your joy.

- Lead with Happiness

  Whether you're a team leader or a solo contributor, your emotional state is contagious. Show others that excellence and well-being can co-exist.

- Give Yourself Permission

  Permission to rest. Permission to say no. Permission to laugh. Permission to redefine success on your terms.

- Reconnect with Your Compass

  Remember my proposed Happiness Compass:

  Happiness = A × (M + E + R + S)

  Keep realigning with your values, mindset, energy, relationships, and small joys.

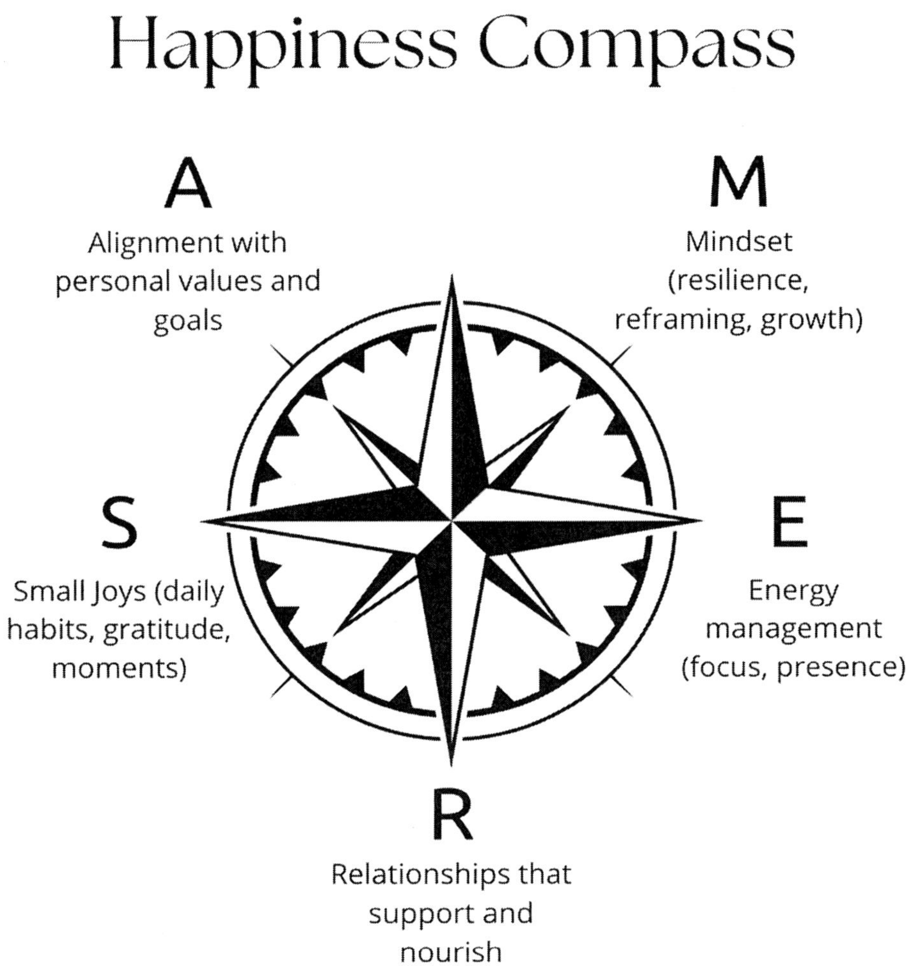

PHYCHOLOGY
SOCIOLOGY
HAPPINESS
NEURO SCIENCE

FORGIVE YOURSELF

LOVE
TIME
SEEDING RELATIONSHIPS

HAPPINESS
GRATITUDE
THANKFULLNESS

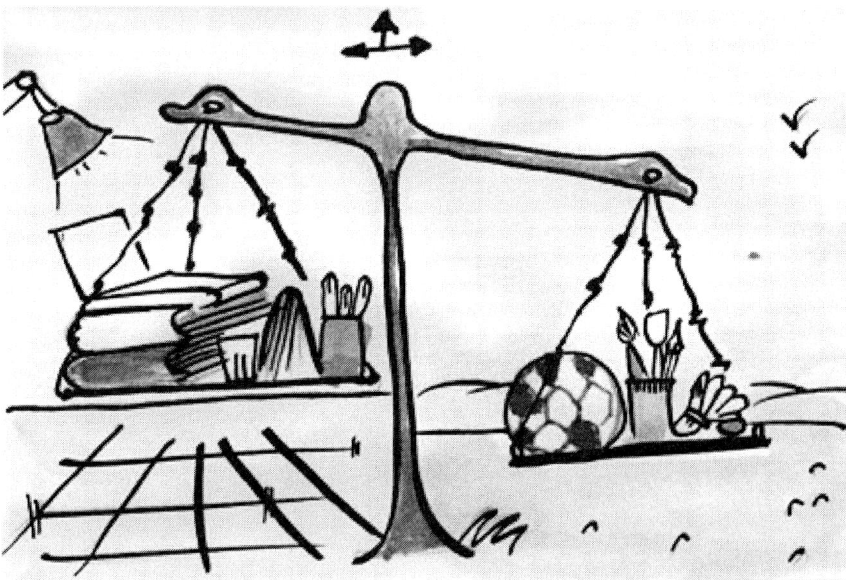

I Forgive You
Are You Forgivingly -Fit

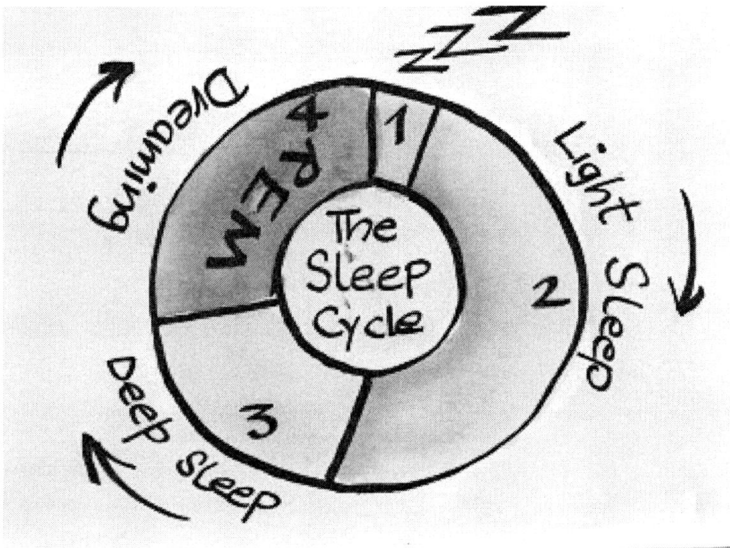
The Sleep Cycle
1
2
3
4 REM
Light Sleep
Deep Sleep
Dreaming
ZZZ

EMOTIONAL HEALTH
MENTAL HEALTH
PHYSICAL HEALTH

A Note from Me for You . . .

This book was born out of my personal quest—watching brilliant, passionate professionals burn out, disconnect, or postpone joy for "someday."

I wrote it for people like you: driven yet human, capable yet stretched, successful yet still searching.

You don't need to change everything to be happy.

You just need to change a few things consistently.

So go ahead—start with 5 minutes a day. Or one small win a week.

That's how transformation begins—not with intensity, but with intentionality.

Wishing you deep happiness,

not someday—but now.

In your work. In your life. In your being.

Dr. Mandeep Sharma
Certified Happiness & Life Coach
Senior Practitioner EMCC
PhD, FIE, Chartered Engineer, PMP, PBA